Bits & Pieces
The Fabric of a Family

D. Jean Yates

2016

Copyright © 2016 D. Jean Yates

All rights reserved.
No part of this book may be reproduced or transmitted in any form or by any means, electronic or mechanical, including photocopying, recording, or by any information storage and retrieval system, without written permission from the author.

ISBN 978-0-692-75539-6
First Edition

Printed in the United States of America

Published and Printed by:

Enlighten Books, LLC
837 Cedar Bough Place
New Albany, Indiana 47150

www.enlightenbooks.com

The Pieces

James Richard Hawkins
1897-1966

Myrtie Belle Sego Hawkins
1910-2002

James Eldred Hawkins
1932 - 2011

Alma Janice Hawkins
1934 - 1980

Hubert Leon Hawkins
1937 - 2015

Charles R. Hawkins
1942 - 2011

Delma Jean Hawkins
1945 -

Nora Belle Hawkins
1949 -

In memory of my parents: James Richard and Myrtie Hawkins; and of my siblings: Jim, Alma, Hubert and Charles Hawkins; and my nephews: Michael Hawkins and Joseph Gault.

For my sons, Barry and Marvin Yates and for their children and grandchildren – Jesse, Christopher, Tyler, Carter, Michael, Joseph, and Jayden.

For my sister, Nora House and my nieces and nephews: Joyce, Judy, Justin, Leona, Tammy, Sarah, John Patrick, Tim, Scott, Adam, and for their children and grandchildren.

May you discover as I have discovered, the family from which we all came – a crazy quilt of characters and experiences, never boring, always challenging, always loved.

– A special thanks to my husband, Roger. His confidence and support are never ending.

A note to my readers

I didn't start out to write a book. After my closest brother, Charles, died of lung cancer in April of 2011, I started writing letters to him as a way to deal with grief.

Each letter was about an incident I remembered from our childhood. Then, my oldest brother, Jim, died four months later in September of 2011. I expanded my letter writing to include him. Then, I just continued writing. Each remembered incident would spur another memory. I wrote letters to my oldest sister, Alma, who died in 1980; to my middle brother, Hubert who died in 2015; and to my only living sibling, my younger sister, Nora.

Soon, I had a stack of letters and thought, "I should turn these into a book."

A note about organization

Before I left my parents' home when I was 16, I had lived in at least 12 different houses. This book is organized with an introduction to each house followed by letters recounting bits and pieces of memory from each.

Some "facts" may not be exact. For example, exactly what date did we move from one place to another? Sometimes, I'm not sure. These are memories, some vague, as recorded in a child's mind. They are as true as I can make them.

The real names of my parents and siblings are used throughout. However, I have changed other names occasionally when reporting a sensitive issue.

A note about grammar

Some grammar "mistakes" are intentional to represent the way my family talked as I was growing up.

To clean up the language would be to change the flavor of our daily lives.

Mom stitching up memories – 1980's

Memory Quilt (for Mom)

Scraps of childhood drape my bed
Remnants of memory pieced together in a
Multi-hued patch work.
Here's a piece of the dress
I wore to 8th grade graduation
And here's a piece of Nora's
And Alma's…
Bits and pieces of varied colors
Bright yellow, pale blue,
Dark brown or black -
Prints and solids
Sewn together with loving stitches,
Bordered by strips of white
Quilted like a vine.

I see you now…
Back hunched over the frame
Hardly lifting your eyes, you quilt
Tiny stitches – over and over – up and down.
A prick of your finger draws blood…
You pause for a moment
Lift finger to mouth
Lick the salty taste of love.

Stitching Together a Family

Like the quilt on my bed
The days of our lives were
Stitched together in bits and pieces -
Dark and brown or bright and cheerful.
Shared DNA and circumstance created a family.

Child by child and
Year by year
Our family grew.
A little sister was born.
An older sister and brother
Got married.
In-laws, nieces, and nephews arrived
adding color and texture.

Then
Alienation. Divorce. Death.
Suddenly I am old.
The quilt of life has grown thin.
I gather up bits and pieces to
Remember who we were…
And the vine
That held us all together.

She called herself Jean...

And it came to pass on May 7, 1945, that a baby girl was born to Richard and Myrtie Hawkins. And she was born in a house called The Round Top in Hart County in Kentucky. Like the four siblings before her and the one to come later, she was born at home because she was of the house and lineage of poor Kentucky farmers. And so it was that Myrtie brought forth her 2nd born daughter. She called her Delma, which means noble protector, and wrapped her in a blanket and placed her in a drawer to be used as a bed.

And when two weeks were accomplished, Richard and Myrtie took the child to church. And the child grew in the church and came to love the music and to follow along in the hymnal. This was her first exposure to written words. And her older sister, Alma, fed this love of music and of words. And Alma taught the child to read the words of the songs they sang.

And when seven years were accomplished, the child started school. And there was a teacher, Ms. K., whose mission it was to teach children of the poor. She nourished the child's mind and taught her to read books. And she taught the child to write the words she read in the books. And the child grew and passed on to second grade where Miss W. continued to nurture her reading and writing. And so it was that each succeeding teacher built on the success of the past. And the child loved school and learning.

But while her mind was nurtured, her emotions were not. And when there was strife within the family, the child Delma, true to her name, became the noble protector of everyone else's feelings and did not acknowledge her own. She retreated into books – into reading and into writing. What she could not say out loud, she wrote in stories and poems.

The child didn't like her name. It felt oppressive. Other children couldn't get it right. They called her Thelma or Delmer. And so it was that when the child changed schools in the fifth grade, she started calling herself Jean, her middle name, which means "God is Gracious."

And the child grew in knowledge and in wisdom. She began to claim the power of her middle name. God in his graciousness helped her to learn that protecting the feelings of others did not mean denying her own. And the child continued to call herself Jean and she became a teacher and began to teach others that which she had learned.

Richard and Myrtie Sego Hawkins – Mom and Daddy

A Strange Pairing

I've often wondered how my parents came to be married. Mom was an unmarried 20 year old from a conservative Southern Baptist family. She was the next to youngest of 10 children. Her parents, William Henry and Nannie Belle Sego, taught their children to attend church and to study the Bible. Two of Mom's brothers, Charles and Thurman, became preachers. Charles spent most of his life as the pastor of a church in Clarksville, Tennessee. Thurman served wherever he felt "called" - mostly at small country churches around Kentucky.

Daddy's parents, Enos and Nora Belle Hawkins, also had a large family. As told to me by Aunt Ida, Daddy and his siblings were also reared as Southern Baptists and taught to respect the church and its teachings. Daddy and Mom met at a revival service in Hart County, Kentucky. Daddy was a 33 year old divorced man who already had a son and a daughter. I can't imagine my Sego grandparents approving of him.

What did Mom's parents think about Daddy? What

did Mom think about Daddy being divorced and already having children? I wish that I could have talked to my mother. But topics like this were never discussed when I was growing up. In fact rarely was anything discussed.

Mom was a very quiet and reserved person and Daddy was always away from the house working. By the time I became old enough and brave enough to talk to Mom about anything important, she was already in the beginning stages of Alzheimer's.

In 1996 Nora and I asked her, "Mom, how did your parents allow you to marry Daddy?" "They couldn't stop me," she replied. Now, this may or may not have been true. The woman I knew as my mother was strong willed but timid. I can't imagine that she would have defied her parents. I can't imagine that she would have married anyone without their consent.

A Good Talking To

Mom was a stay-at-home mom who tended her children, her house and her gardens. Reared on a Baptist teaching of not being proud or boastful, Mom had difficulty accepting compliments. I often thought that her humility was misplaced. She had many talents. Perhaps her greatest talent was turning a house into a home. She had a lot of practice doing that as Daddy was constantly moving the family from one place to another.

When Daddy was killed in an accident in 1966, he and Mom had been married for 36 years. They had lived in 14 houses and never in any one house for longer than 5 years. Each time she moved, Mom would scrub the house clean, make curtains, and plant flower gardens. Her attitude seemed to be "we may not be here long but I want this to feel like home."

Clearly Mom had the talent to discipline us children without ever spanking us and with rarely raising her voice. Her method of choice was to give us a "good talking to." Anytime we misbehaved she'd warn, "You better straighten up or I'm going to give you a good talking to." If we were out in public, maybe in church or at the grocery store, she'd give us a look that said, "You better behave or I'm going to take you home and give you a good talking to." The look and the talking to were the sternest discipline I ever received. They worked in stopping the targeted behavior but left me with a lingering burden of guilt. I would have much preferred a spanking.

As an adult, I have come to believe that lingering guilt is a wasted emotion. It robs one of energy and spirit. But, imparting a sense of guilt seemed to be the one most employed by Baptists and other conservative religions in the 1950's. I came to envy my Catholic friends, who confessed, did their penance and went on with life. I carried my guilt with me.

Poor Do

When I was growing up in various places in rural Kentucky, life was very different than it is today. I was the 8th child (Daddy had 2 children before he married Mom) of a farmer with a 5th grade education who also worked "public" work to provide a meager existence for his family.

Most of our neighbors, wherever we lived, were similar to us. We had shelter and enough to eat. We were luckier than many because Daddy and Mom grew a huge garden and often times raised and butchered their own pigs. They usually kept a few chickens for eggs and for an occasional meal of baked or fried chicken.

Mom was a talented country cook. She could make a tasty meal to feed a family from what some folks would throw out to the pigs. One of her best dishes, made when provisions were particularly low, was called "Poor-Do."

It was made with bacon grease, crumbled corn bread, chopped green onions, and gravy made from flour and milk. Thinking of it now, it reminds me of stove top stuffing only better. I used to think she called it "Poor-Do" as a way of saying, "This is what the poor do when they can do nothing else."

I have come to realize that it was probably just a phrase she used to describe most of her efforts. She had difficulty accepting compliments. Whenever someone complemented her on a quilt she had made or a cake she had baked, she'd always say, "Ah, this is a poor do."

Mom was also a talented seamstress. With only a basic pattern used to help her size the garment, she made clothes for Nora and me from feed sacks (printed cotton sacks that came packed with feed for the animals).

She could look at a picture of a dress in a Sears-Roebuck catalog and produce one very similar. She could also remake clothes that were handed down to us by people with whom Daddy worked or by other people in the community or the church we attended. Even altering coats was not beyond her skills. Consequently, it was several years before I realized we were "poor".

On the Move

I used to think that the one constant in my life was change. From the earliest I can remember we were always on the move. By the time I left home at the age of 16, I had lived in at least 12 different houses. I'm not sure why we moved so much.

As a child, I thought that Daddy just had itchy feet. With a grown up's perspective, I now think that he was always trying to better himself and our family. He was mostly a tenant farmer who also worked public work.

The first house I know of that he actually owned was the house we lived in on Ford Highway.

All our houses had a name. Kind of like naming a pet, I guess. We lived in so many different houses, we had to have some way to distinguish one from the other. Much easier to say, "Old Butch" than to say, "The old brown dog we had when we lived in Grayson County." Much easier to say, "44" than to say the house we lived in when Nora was born.

Anyway, we referred to each house by the road it was on, or by its peculiar architecture, or the community it was in, or by the name of the person who owned it.

I was born in the "Round-Top," a house near Cub Run in Hart County, Kentucky. According to my parents, the house had unusual architecture that lent the roof a somewhat circular shape. I can't imagine how it looked and have been unable to locate any pictures. Recently, while trying to locate it, I learned that it had been torn down and something else built in its place.

From the Round Top, my family moved to Logsdon Valley, still in Hart County. We lived in Logsdon Valley for about a year and then moved to Big Clifty in Grayson County. After Big Clifty, we moved to Bennett's Hog Farm in Bullitt County, then to 44, also in Bullitt County.

Next it was on to Hardin County where we lived in seven different houses: The Guess Place, The Grimes Place, Ford Highway, Cecilia 1 (by the gas storage facility), Cecilia 2 (by the railroad), Cecilia 3 (the Peter's House) and Cecilia 4 (the New House).

After I left home, my parents lived in at least five additional houses.

My earliest memories are from Big Clifty.

Big Clifty
A Rustle in the Grass

Although I couldn't have been more than three years old, I have some vague memories of our life in Big Clifty.

We had a dog named Butch. Butch killed a rather large rattlesnake and Daddy cut off and saved the rattle – five buttons long. For years Mom kept the rattle in a small white box, like that in which a piece of jewelry might be kept. At some point in time, she gave the box to me. I kept the box until the rattle eventually disintegrated.

The story of "Old Butch" (as Butch was affectionately called) and the rattlesnake was repeated often in our family. It went something like this.

Daddy was working, clearing brush from the fence row of the property on which we lived. Old Butch, as always, was tagging along beside him. Suddenly, Old Butch started barking – not a friendly bark as he would make if a neighbor or someone else were approaching. This was a frantic bark as if he were trying to warn Daddy of something.

As the bark became louder and more insistent, Daddy paused in his work. "What in the world is this dog barking at?" he wondered. Then he heard a rustle in the brush near where he was standing and looked down to see a large rattlesnake coiled and ready to strike. Before Daddy could move, Old Butch pounced. He caught the snake in his mouth and backed up slinging it back and forth. When Old Butch finally released the snake, Daddy chopped its head off with the same ax he had been using to clear brush. Sitting down on a nearby stump to recover his composure, he realized that Old Butch had probably saved his life.

"Come on, Old Butch. Let's go back to the house," he said. "We both need a fresh drink."

Although Daddy didn't usually allow dogs into the house, this time he made an exception. Old Butch came in and didn't leave Daddy's side for the remainder of the day. From that day forward, Old Butch was allowed inside any time he wanted.

This story was repeated in our family for years. Old Butch became more heroic and the rattlesnake grew bigger and bigger each time the story was told.

Big Clifty
Under the Table

Another memory from Big Clifty is a bit more clear.

A new road was being built near our house. Charles and I were intrigued with all the large machines – road graders, dump trucks, and digging equipment. Each day we'd stand at the window or at the edge of our yard and watch for hours. As time passed and we became braver, we'd inch a little nearer to the work site.

"Stay in your yard." Mom repeatedly warned us. "You could get hurt over there with all that big equipment."

One day, we drifted off a bit farther, not even noticing when we left our yard. We forgot time as we watched the big dump trucks and road graders hypnotically moving back and forth and back and forth.

Then, as if from a long distance, we heard Mom. "Charles!" she called. "Sissy! Where are you?" She must have been frantic when she looked out and didn't see us.

My brother Charles and me enjoying fresh watermelon – Summer of 1946.

Mom NEVER yelled. Now, we became frantic.

Knowing that we were in big trouble, we scurried back into the house and tried to hide under the kitchen table. Mom, of course, found us. "Come out from under there!" she said sternly. Feeling guilty and a little bit afraid, we crept out.

Although Mom had never even spanked us, we both knew we were going to get a whipping this time. But, we were wrong. She just gave us "a good talking to." We felt really bad that we had let Mom down and caused her to worry.

But, that new road was still being built… the sound of the big equipment still called to us. "Come on over. come on over," it seemed to say. "You can get a much better look over here."

Each time we were tempted, we'd hear Mom's voice, "Stay in the yard, kids. Stay near the house where I can see you." We'd remember the "good talking to" from our last excursion and creep right to the yard's edge. We'd sit there for hours, hypnotized.

Bennett's Hog Farm
"Made in the U.S.A."

Soon after the incident with the road building equipment, our family moved to Bullitt County. We first lived on the Bennett Hog Farm. Here we were given reduced rent for helping to take care of the hogs. Daddy continued to work at various places, usually at one service station or another.

I have vague memories of living on Bennett's farm. Our family became close friends with the Stockdale family. Ginny Stockdale and Alma, my older sister, often got together in the evening and made chocolate fudge and vinegar taffy. Also, I vaguely remember a story about bananas.

As Mom told it, sometimes when Daddy had a little extra money, he would buy a stalk of bananas. My siblings and I evidently didn't like bananas all that much. When it looked as though some of them would go bad before they were eaten, Mom gave them to the Stockdales. Invariably,

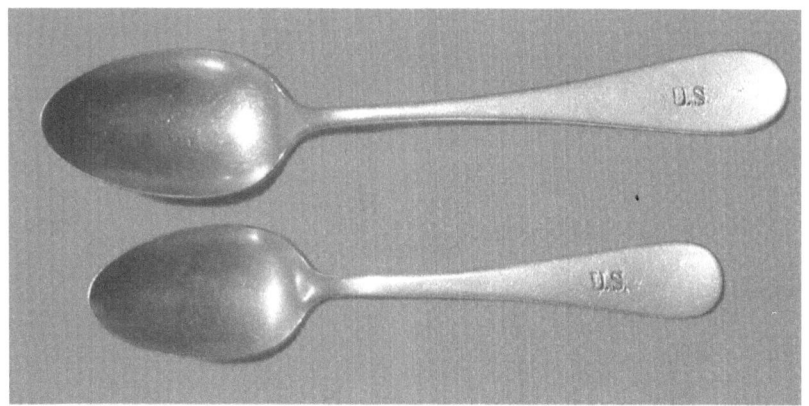

she would go into their home later and catch us eating those same bananas. They must have tasted better there than they had in our own kitchen!

It was also on the hog farm where we collected eating utensils. Periodically a truck from Fort Knox delivered slop (food left over from feeding the soldiers and collected and saved as slop for the hogs) to the farm.

Sometimes, table utensils, carelessly discarded by soldiers, could be found in the hog trough. We collected and cleaned them and those utensils were probably the best quality tableware Mom ever owned.

I and other family members still have a few pieces – marked on the back with the words "Stainless Steel – made in the USA" and on the front with "U.S." in large capital letters.

Forty-four

From Bennett's farm, we moved to a small frame house sitting on a hill or knob beside Highway 44 in Bullitt County. This was the fifth house in which I'd lived in my four years of life.

We lived on 44 for about a year when I was four. We didn't own 44, but rather rented it. 44 was a small house with no indoor plumbing and no electricity. We drew our water from a cistern, a storage tank where rainwater was collected and saved, located just outside the kitchen door on a screened porch. During dry periods with little rain, a large tanker truck brought water and filled the cistern. When nature called, we went to the outhouse in the back yard. For light, we used kerosene lamps. For heat and for cooking, we used wood stoves.

Daily living was labor intense. Wood was cut and brought in to fuel the stoves. Then a fire was started. Starting the fires required kindling, technique and patience. The kitchen stove was usually kept hot all day. Meals were

Alma sitting on car in front of our house on 44.

cooked and eaten at home – there was no running down the street to pick up a burger or pizza. "Eating out" meant carrying our food into the yard and sitting under a shade tree while we ate.

Laundry was done once each week and consumed an entire day. It was done in two galvanized tubs in the side yard. On laundry day, water for the wash was heated and the tubs were filled. The boys, Jim, Hubert, and Charles, filled and emptied the tubs as needed. Mom and Alma dunked clothes in a tub of soapy water and used a scrub board to scrub the clothes clean. Then, they rinsed the clothes in a second tub and wrung them out by hand to remove as much water as possible before hanging them on the clothes line (a heavy wire stretched between two posts in the back yard) to dry.

Everyone helped on laundry day. Even I, a four year old, helped by handing clothes pins to Mom or to Alma as they hung clothes on the line. When the clothes were dry, I helped again by carrying a bag and collecting the pins as the clothes were taken down.

Children were expected to contribute to the family by doing whatever needed to be done. We didn't get allowances or pay for doing chores. Our pay was food, clothing, a bed – and the confidence gained by being a contributing member of our family.

Forty-four
Best Friends

Living on 44 was fun for me.

The Clonnor family lived behind us in a house similar to ours. Emily Clonnor, the youngest child in their family, and I were about the same age. We played together constantly.

We'd spend almost every summer afternoon pushing each other in the rope swing hung from a big tree in our front yard. When we became tired of swinging, we'd hold hands and circle around and around until we became dizzy. We'd fall down in a fit of giggles, sit for a while on the ground and then get back up and do it all again.

The Clonnor family must have had a little more money than our family and frequently bought treats for the children. Emily always had gum and I never did. So, when Emily came to play in our yard, she would chew her gum a while and then give it to me and I'd chew a while. When Mom realized what we were doing, she was really upset.

Just as she had done many times, she gave me another "good talking to." "Don't chew other people's gum," she said. "There's no telling what germs you could get or what disease you might catch."

Fear of germs and disease was not a concept I understood. But gum chewing, now that was real.

Temptation was too great and Emily and I continued to share. I tried to remember not to chew when Mom was around. Or, if I did have gum in my mouth and saw her coming, I'd quickly take it out or swallow it.

Emily was my first best friend.

Forty-four
Mean Kids

Dear Jim,

Some of my first memories of you are when we lived on 44. I was only four years old but I clearly remember some of your shenanigans.

Do you remember the Clonnor children who lived next door to us? One day Johnny and Emily had been in our yard playing with Charles and me. We all became tired and hot and went inside to cool off. Space inside was very limited – especially seating space. You were home and sitting on the couch. Charles and I quickly claimed spots beside you. The Clonnor kids, Johnny and Emily, plopped down on the floor.

We sat and talked and joked until I had to leave the room to get a drink of water. Getting up from the couch, I announced, "Don't anyone take my spot while I'm gone.".

Of course, as soon as I stepped away, Johnny jumped from the floor and into "my" spot. He didn't so much want to sit on the sofa as he wanted to aggravate me.

When I came back into the room, Johnny refused to give my spot back. You, as the protective big brother, told him to get up. When he refused, you stood up and put his head in a choke hold. Then you put it on the sofa and sat on it.

"So, big boy, you still want to sit here?" you said, chuckling.

"No. Let me up!" Johnny replied.

"Have you learned your lesson?"

"Yes" he mumbled.

"What's that? I can't hear you," you said as you loosened your choke hold.

"Yes!" Johnny repeated in a louder voice as he stood and nodded his head up and down. Then he took Emily by the hand and led her to the door.

"Let's go home," he said. "These kids are mean."

Forty-four
"Enough of that..."

Dear Daddy,

"That's enough of that!" are the first specific words I remember hearing you say.

I was 4 years old, the baby of the family. It was a typical summer afternoon in early July. I had spent the morning playing with my best friend Emily. Do you remember her?

She and her family lived just up the hill behind us. We'd swung in the tree swing in our yard, traded chewing gum, played Ring Around the Rosie and worn ourselves out. When I became hot and tired, I went inside to be with Mom. She wiped my sweaty face and dirty hands with a cool wash cloth. Then, after a glass of lemonade, she and I snuggled down on the bed for a nap.

Mom and I were home alone. You were at work at a gas station in Jefferson County. The older siblings, Jim,

Alma, Hubert and Charles were somewhere doing what older children did at the time – hanging out at the nearby country store with their friends or working in someone's tobacco or just traipsing around in the knobby fields that surrounded us.

You came home in the early afternoon just as we had gotten comfortable and I had dozed off to sleep. I heard a door open and felt Mom move away from me. Still half asleep, I started to whine and to hold on to Mom. I didn't want her to get up.

You wanted Mom to get up and fix some lunch. In 1949, times were different than they are now. When a man wanted food, the woman went to the kitchen and prepared it. Mom was several months pregnant with Nora.

Yet, when you asked for lunch, she didn't hesitate. As she left me on the bed, my whining continued and soon turned into sobs. That's when you spoke to me. "Sissy, be quiet" you said. "Go back to sleep."

Crankily, I continued to cry and sob even louder. Why? I don't know. Maybe I just didn't get my nap out. Maybe I was a bit spoiled and didn't like it when I didn't get my way. Maybe I sensed that my time of being the baby of the family would soon be over and that my napping days with Mom were about to come to an end.

Whatever the reason, I couldn't stop crying.

"That's enough of that, Sissy," you said again in your sternest voice. "Stop your crying and go back to sleep." But, I couldn't stop crying. I continued to lie on the bed sobbing. Warm salty tears trickled down my face. Choking sobs escaped my throat. Then, as if my entire body were crying, I felt a wet, warm sensation seeping around my legs. A circle of moisture appeared on the bed. The reason I had started to cry was no longer important. I now continued to cry because I had wet the bed and was too embarrassed to let you know.

"That's enough of that, Sissy." I heard you say again in an aggravated, impatient voice. "If you don't stop that crying, I'll give you something to cry about." Those words, and the tone in which you said them, only made me cry more. Then you picked me up, turned me over your knee, and spanked me. You put me in a chair near the table where you sat to eat your lunch. My tears gradually subsided and my sobs turned into sniffles.

After you finished lunch and went outside, Mom changed my clothes and took the wet sheet from the bed. She snuggled back down with me until I was quiet and calm and drifting back to sleep.

You never spanked me again after that day.

Forty-four
Surprise!

Dear Nora,

I was 4 years old. We lived in a small house on Highway 44 in Bullitt County. That evening Mom sent Charles and me to the Clonnor's house. We didn't know what was going on. Although we played with the Clonnor children often during the day, it was usually in our yard and we were never sent to theirs.

I don't remember many specifics about that night. But, after Charles and I left, a doctor came to our house. He arrived just in time to deliver you at home under the flickering light of a kerosene lamp. After what seemed like hours, Charles and I were called back home. Boy, were we surprised!

There you were – a red, wrinkly, squirmy baby. Everyone seemed happy and pleased. I didn't know what to think but I guessed I'd try to be happy, too. I had already become a "pleaser" and didn't want to upset anyone.

Days passed.

Mom and Daddy and our older siblings gave you lots of attention - too much attention for me, a four year old, to understand.

"What's so special about this baby?" I thought. "The only thing she does is cry and nurse then poop and sleep." I kept these thoughts to myself and just smiled in reluctant agreement as others swooned over you and talked about your cuteness. I, who was the one doted on for 4 years, couldn't understand why the focus had changed. I didn't understand why everyone talked about how cute you were and spent more time with you than with me.

As Mom recovered from giving birth, we all had to pitch in and do more than our normal share around the house. Hubert and Alma did much of the cooking. Jim helped to keep things straightened up, to bring in wood for the cooking stove and to do other chores. Charles and I did what we could – setting the table, drying the dishes, whatever we were asked to do.

I gradually began to accept the new baby and to gain confidence in my role as the "big sister." We continued to play with the Clonnor children and I started to feel proud and began to brag about "my" new baby.

Forty-four
A Family Picture

Dear Nora,

Charles and I were surprised by your birth.

We were too young to understand beforehand that Mom was going to have a baby. Not long after you arrived, we got another surprise.

As a family, we rarely went anywhere. But, when you were only a few weeks old, we took a trip to see Aunt Mae, Daddy's youngest sister. She and her family lived on a farm outside Indianapolis, Indiana. To make a trip from Bullitt County, Kentucky, to Indianapolis was a big deal and took a lot of planning and saving. But, Daddy and Mom were eager to show off the latest addition to our family.

The drive to Aunt Mae's was uneventful. Upon our arrival, you of course, gained many new admirers. We only stayed for the weekend but that was long enough for our Indiana kin to fall in love with you - the new baby named

Hawkins Family Picture, Summer, 1949, visiting Aunt Mae.

Nora Belle, after Grandma Hawkins, Daddy's and Aunt Mae's mother.

Late on Sunday afternoon of that visit, Daddy packed up the car for the return trip home. We all gathered around to say good-bye. One of my favorite family pictures is the one Aunt Mae took of us before we left. It is a picture of our entire family grouped beside our car. It is the only picture I can locate of you as a baby.

If I could go back and freeze our family in time, it would be the time during which this picture was taken. The core family was complete and intact. Outside influences in the form of sons-in-law or daughters-in-law had not yet intruded.

In this picture, we are healthy and happy. Mom and Daddy are both smiling and looking proud. Dressed in typical work clothes and wearing a hat, Daddy towers above all. Standing beside him Mom holds you securely wrapped in a blanket. Hubert and Jim are dressed in their "Sunday go to meeting" clothes and Alma is looking very stylish and mature for a 14 year old. Charles is standing straight with a proud and serious take charge look on his face.

I'm the little girl in front with her hand to her mouth. I am shy and insecure and still have mixed feelings about this new baby who seems to get everyone's attention. Sure,

I'm proud but also a little bit jealous. "Hey, I'm still here. I'm still cute," I want to say. Has everyone forgotten about me?

Forty-four
Pretty Boy

Dear Jim,

Do you remember moving day when we moved from 44? Nora was only a few months old and I was 4.

You were a teenager who hadn't been driving very long. You were, as the kids say today, a "chick magnet" with dark curly hair and a friendly smile. You were not exactly modest about your good looks nor shy about showing off. Some of the teenage boys teased you. "Look at pretty boy," they'd say. But you would just laugh as girls gathered round.

Things were hectic that day as we all worked to get the moving truck loaded. The morning passed and everyone was hungry. Daddy sent you to a nearby store to pick up some bread and bologna to make sandwiches for lunch. Of course, the rest of us kids also piled into the car.

I sat in the back next to one of the doors of our four door Chevy. In case there were any girls around to impress, you started showing off your driving skills, popping wheelies and taking the curves too fast. Just before we got to the store, we rounded a curve and the back door came open. I fell out. You stopped the car and jumped out to help me. "Are you hurt? Is anything broken?" you asked in a worried voice. "No. I'm o.k. Just a little skinned place on my arm," I said. I was a little embarrassed about falling out so probably wouldn't have told you even if I were hurt.

Letting out a relieved sigh, you brushed me off, checked my arms and legs to see if they still worked and helped me back into the car. As we continued on to the store, you drove a little more responsibly. You bought the lunch supplies; then we headed home. You expected to be in trouble when Mom and Daddy learned what had happened. But, when we arrived back home, everyone was too busy to notice anything. You and I ate our lunch in silence with an occasional glance of conspiracy that seemed to say, "I won't tell if you won't."

You didn't get in trouble. We moved and my arm healed. You started to drive a little more responsibly, even when there were girls around to impress.

The Guess Place

From 44, we moved to "The Guess Place". It must have been owned by someone named Guess.

The Guess Place was located at the end of a dirt lane off Springfield Road in Hardin County. The house was hardly more than a shack with only three rooms. It was heated by a fireplace and a kitchen stove. There wasn't room for a heating stove.

As I imagine the house now, I think of worn linoleum on the floor and wallpaper more like utilitarian heavy brown paper to keep out the wind. The outside was gray weathered boards that had never been painted. Eight of us – Mom, Daddy, and six children – lived there together.

The lane leading to the house was about ¼ mile long. It was nothing more than ruts worn out over time by wagons or other farm equipment. During periods of heavy rain or snow, the lane became muddy and almost impossible to maneuver. Daddy's car frequently became stuck in the mud and the older boys helped him to push it out

The big plus of living on the Guess Place was that

it had more land space. There was room for a vegetable garden, a few cows, and a tobacco crop. There was a barn to shelter the cows and to house the tobacco once it was cut. There was no well or cistern but rather a fresh water spring located at the bottom of a hill behind our house.

Charles and I were assigned the task of getting water from the spring. We didn't mind because we could loiter and explore. Though I was only five and Charles eight, we liked the responsibility of keeping fresh water in the house. Traipsing down the hill was fun. We felt important and grown up.

We settled into the Guess Place rather quickly. I missed the Clonnor children, especially Emily. But I had my siblings and we never lacked imagination. We found lots of ways to entertain ourselves.

Because there were no close neighbors, Charles and I became closer as friends. We bonded over our mutual suspicion of Nora and all the attention she kept getting. Daddy, as usual, was always working. We didn't see him very much.

I thought it was normal for fathers to be always dressed in overalls or work clothes and to be always out working. With no television and no shows like "Father Knows Best" depicting the perfect middle class family, the way we lived was the only way we knew. We had almost no material comforts but we were happy.

The Guess Place
The Move

Dear Hubert,

"I tell you, you ought to have seen us. We must have looked like the Beverly Hillbillies broke down in an old truck beside the highway." That's the way you started the story about our move from 44 to the Guess Place. Laughing, you settled back in your chair and continued.

"You remember Uncle Vince, Dad's brother. He had an old Chevy truck and helped move us from Bullitt County. We loaded up everything we owned and tied it on that truck so it wouldn't blow away. Somewhere between Ft. Knox and E-town the truck stopped running. It took all three of us to push it to the side of the road out of the way of other traffic."

"Well, we finally got it off the highway and Uncle Vince tried to start it again. He cranked the engine so much that Dad kept saying, 'Vince, you're going to run the battery down.' I kept trying to get Dad's attention, pulling on the leg of his pants and saying, 'I have an idea.' Well, you know how Dad was. He didn't listen to nobody. So, Vince and Dad kept tinkering around under the hood but couldn't get the truck started."

"After a while I was about to bust wanting to say something. 'Maybe we've run out of gas,' I blurted out. They didn't believe me, of course, but they hadn't had any luck with anything else. Dad poked around in the back of the truck and found a beat up gas can."

"Just about that time some old man stopped and took me and Dad down the road a piece to a service station. Dad used the last dollar in his pocket to buy gas – about 4 gallons, I think. Then the old man took us back to our truck. He stayed with us while Dad put the gas in the gas tank and told Vince to 'crank it up.' The truck started on the first try. After Dad thanked the old man, we climbed back into our truck. Dad laid his arm up on the back of the seat kind of around my shoulders. 'Good job, son' he said."

"Well, it was about dark when we finally got home to the Guess Place. You know how Dad almost never bragged on me. He usually was fussing at me for something. So, as he told everyone about why we was late and about how it was my idea to check the gas tank, I just stood there with a silly grin on my face and didn't say a word. It felt good to make Daddy proud."

The Guess Place
Yummy!

Dear Hubert,

I will always remember your birthday in 1950.

We were living at the Guess Place. I was only 5 but I loved to "help" Mom cook. Unlike some mothers, she never shooed me out of the kitchen or acted as if I were in her way.

One day she asked, "Sissy, how would you like to make a cake?" She gathered the ingredients and after showing me how to measure the milk, butter, and sugar, she taught me to carefully break the eggs. In no time, I was struggling to mix all the ingredients together. Didn't have electric mixers then. Didn't even have electricity. Just had to stir away with a large spoon and scrape the sides of the mixing bowl occasionally with another spoon.

By the time we had the cake ready to put into the oven, "I was plum tuckered out" as you used to say. I was proud though. It was a special cake. Baked in a black iron skillet in the oven of an old wood cooking stove, the cake turned out a little lopsided. But, I evened it out with butter cream frosting that Mom made. It was beautiful. I could hardly wait to show it to you!

"Happy Birthday to you, Happy Birthday to you..." we all sang that night after supper while I held the cake and you blew out the candles – all 13 of them. "This is the best cake I've ever eaten," you said, smiling at me with frosting on your face. Then everyone else had a piece and kept saying, "Yum. This is the best cake ever!" Though those words were possibly an exaggeration, the compliments fed my ego and I was eager to keep on baking.

I still like to bake cakes but now I mix and beat the ingredients with an electric mixer. Baked in the oven of an electric range, they turn out smooth and pretty. None are ever as tasty, though, as that first cake I baked "by myself" in December of 1950.

The Guess Place
A Living Machine

Dear Jim,

I sure wish you were here to tell my children and grandchildren about the tobacco crop Daddy put in while we lived on the Guess Place.

The potential for a good tobacco crop is one of the main things that drew Daddy to the place. He was always looking for a way to make money.

More than the tobacco itself, I remember the cutting. You were already working part-time at various spots around Elizabethtown. Hubert was thirteen and Charles eight.

They had helped to set the tobacco and to keep the weeds chopped out as it was growing but neither was strong enough to help very much with the cutting.

Daddy was always working a full time job and trying to farm some at the same time, so he had to hire someone to help. I'm not sure where he found him, but on a dry sunny

Richard Hawkins' family working in tobacco about 1946. Even young children were expected to help.

day in late August, Knot Head Berry showed up.

I suppose his last name was Berry although I don't know for sure. He had a large growth on the side of his forehead, so everyone just called him "Knot Head".

This was way before the time of trying to be politically or socially correct. Practically everyone had a nickname and no one took offense easily. Knot Head didn't seem to mind what Daddy or anyone else called him.

You always could tell a good story. I can almost hear you chuckle as you describe Knot Head. "Why man," you'd say. "He was a living machine. And he didn't have to warm up neither. No. Old Knot Head came in the morning ready to work. He didn't stand around drinking coffee and shooting the breeze like some of these yokels do today."

"With a tobacco knife in one hand, he was like a mad man running up and down those rows. He'd catch a tobacco plant in one hand and bend it over. Then he'd give it one hack with the knife and be off to the next plant. Someone would follow behind and spear the stalks onto a tobacco stick. When he came to the end of a row, he'd skip over one and cut the next row going back. He skipped a row so as not to get in the way of the ones spearing the tobacco."

"He repeated the pattern over and over never wasting any time. No one could keep up with Knot Head. No sir!"

You'd chuckle again as you got to the end of your story. "Can't none of these yokels today, young or old, work like he did. Why they wouldn't last an hour. No sir! They don't make 'em like Knot Head anymore."

The Guess Place Fat Gets Cold

Dear Hubert,

You were always the story teller; you especially liked telling stories about yourself and Jim. One of your favorite stories was about stripping tobacco. It went something like this:

"Jim and I were both just kids. But we were expected to do men's work even when we was young. Jim was five years older than I was so he always thought he was the boss.

"Well, this one day me and Jim was stripping tobacco in an old open barn. I was a little bit chubby and Jim was thin and brawny. We'd been in the barn for a good while and I was getting cold.

"I'm cold, let's go to the house," I kept begging. Jim got aggravated with my whining.

"When we finish the stack of tobacco on the stripping table, we'll take a break and go to the house to warm up," he said impatiently.

"But I was colder by the minute. Acting like a little smart aleck I taunted, "Fat gets cold, skinny don't!" Then I ducked under the table to make my escape. Well, Jim jumped the table and caught me.

"Hubert, I told you'd we'd warm up when we finished the stack on the table!" he declared. Then, just to show me he could, he pushed me back around to the stripping side.

"After a bit of wrestling around, Jim got the best of me.

"Now dag-gum-it! Is the little fat boy warm enough to go ahead and strip this stack?" he asked.

Hubert, you laughed as you told me this story. I don't think you and Jim were ever really angry with each other. You remained good friends until the day he died.

The Guess Place
Robe of Many Colors

Dear Charles,

Living on the Guess Place was fun for me even though you and I always seemed to look for trouble. If it wasn't falling down and skinning a knee or fighting bumblebees or catching ourselves on fire, we were always in trouble. But life was never boring.

Do you remember sleeping on a pallet near the fireplace? Soon after we moved there, I was wearing a flannel robe given to me by someone who worked with Daddy.

Like Joseph's coat, this was a robe of many colors. It was pretty and warm and snuggly. I loved wearing it even though the sleeves were a little long.

One morning, I woke up cold and scooted too close to the fire. Daddy had added wood and was poking around the coals to get the fire going. As he poked, coals popped and sparks flew. One coal popped out and caught the sleeve of my robe on fire. Mom quickly smothered the flames before they could spread.

Good thing that robe wasn't made of some synthetic fabric like most clothes are now. That sleeve would have melted or who knows what else. But, the robe was made of 100% cotton flannel. My arm wasn't even burned.

I continued to wear the robe (with a burn hole in the sleeve) until I outgrew it. Haven't ever had another one that I liked as well.

The Guess Place Bumble Bee Dance

Dear Charles,

Do you remember that first summer after we moved to the Guess Place.? You and I were always running around and playing in the yard. I will never forget that day when you and I were playing tag and made the bumblebees mad.

The house was our home base.

Whenever you were "It" and I thought you were about to catch me, I'd run back and hit the side of the house signaling that I was safe. Or, if I was "It", you ran and hit the side of the house. We didn't know that bumble bees had a nest inside the wall.

That day we played a little too long and a little too rough, I guess. We both hit the house several times and must have made the bees angry. They swarmed out and flew around us. Jumping around and flinging our arms, we must have looked like we were doing an "Indian War Dance" as Mom sometimes said. I think we should call it "The Bumble Bee Dance." Anyway, we ran for the door dancing as we ran.

You managed to get inside to safety but I was stung twice before making it in and slamming the door. Mom took over. Seems like she was always having to take over something.

Anyway, she cleaned my arm with cool water. Then, she made a paste of baking soda and water and smoothed it over the stings. "You'll be all right," she said. "In a couple of days you won't even remember that you were stung."

She was right. My stings healed quickly and I didn't want to go near those bees again. It wasn't necessary for Mom to warn us, "Stay away from that side of the house."

The Guess Place
White Bread & Margarine

Dear Charles,

Do you remember the time we were getting ready to go to visit Grandma and Grandpa Sego who were living with Uncle Tom and Aunt Sarilda in Glendale?

We were excited to go there because they always had white bread and margarine. At home we only ate homemade biscuits and fresh baked cornbread. We never had margarine.

Mom mostly made the biscuits but we all helped to churn our own butter. Mom would let a bucket of fresh milk set until the cream rose to the top. Then she'd skim the cream off and pour it into a large jar. We'd take turns shaking the jar until the cream turned into butter. Mom would turn the butter out onto a plate and shape it into a mound.

Watching the cream as it turned to butter seemed

like magic to us. But, the magic wasn't as good as margarine on white bread. That's what we thought. We always got excited when we knew we were going to visit relatives who had margarine, those yellow sticks of goodness that came from the store.

That day, I was the first to get ready. "Be careful, Sissy. Try not to get dirty." Mom warned me as I ran out of the house. Skipping along, I forgot all about Mom's warning. After all, I was only 5 years old and already tasting the treat that waited for us. How could she expect me to "be careful"?

"Hurry up, Charles," I called to you as I skipped along with thoughts of bread and margarine whirling in my head.

Then it happened. I tripped over a rut in the road and fell, ripping my dress and cutting my knee. Seeing the blood on my knee shocked me so much that I didn't even cry. Heading back to the house I was a disheveled mess expecting to be scolded, or at least to get a good talking to.

But, Mom didn't scold me. She just brushed me off then cleaned and bandaged my knee. She knew when and when not to use "the good talking to". Soon, we were all on our way to Grandma's. I will never forget that day – I still have a scar on my knee to remind me.

The Guess Place
Merry Christmas!

Dear Charles,

I sure wish you were here to help me get my facts straight.

I've been thinking about Christmas when we were children. Christmas then was certainly very different from now. Do you remember our first Christmas at the Guess Place? I believe it was the Christmas of 1949 when Nora was just a baby; I was four and you were seven.

You and I were excited about the new place and really excited about Christmas. We knew that Santa didn't often visit poor kids. But we could still hope. Maybe this would be the year he'd find us. After all, we did have a chimney now and a fireplace too.

Anyway, we were never too disappointed. We knew that on Christmas morning, we'd find oranges and small bags of Chocolate Drops or Peppermint Candy. Any toys or other gifts would just be a bonus.

That Christmas morning we woke up early and ran to see if anything had been left during the night.

Sure enough, along with the oranges and candy, we found three small gifts: one for Nora, one for me, and one for you. Wanting to hold on to a feeling of expectation a little longer, we were reluctant to open them. But Mom told us to go ahead and see what was inside.

Nora got a small white hen that "laid an egg" when someone pushed on its back. I got a small paper accordion or music box as some people called it. And you, you got a plastic horn, kind of like a piccolo.

We were soon making music all over the house. I danced around and played my accordion. You wouldn't put the horn down. More than trying to make music, I think you liked slipping up behind Hubert and tooting that horn to startle him. Then you'd laugh and run away.

Like everywhere we had lived, the house on the Guess Place had no running water. We got water from a spring at the bottom of a small hill behind our house. We didn't even know that some people got their water from a faucet in the kitchen. If anyone had told us, we wouldn't have believed it.

A day or two after Christmas, Mom sent us to the spring. We took our music with us and marched along as though we were leading a parade.

Then, as we came to a rocky incline, you tripped and broke your horn. I continued to play my accordion for a few days but didn't really have the heart for it. If you couldn't make music, I didn't want to either.

Soon, my accordion was torn and useless. Nora's hen, on the other hand, kept on laying those eggs!

The Guess Place Glamorous Sister

Dear Alma,

You were only fifteen when we moved to the Guess Place, but you were already glamorous.

You wore your long dark hair swept back and held in place with combs. You arched your eyebrows and accented them with an eyebrow pencil. You had pale green eyes and long lashes emphasized with mascara. You had dimples and a warm smile accented with red lipstick.

You looked like a movie star.

It really didn't matter how you dressed. Whether wearing a pair of Jim's blue jeans cinched at the waist with grass string or wearing your Sunday best, you were beautiful.

When you started working and earning your own money, you began to buy clothes and jewelry that made you look like a model. You'd wear flowing skirts and dangling rhinestone earrings.

My glamorous sister, Alma.

You had an innate ability to choose and wear glamorous fashions.

You always had a personality and mind of your own. Do you remember how Mom and Daddy used to scold you about plucking your eyebrows and using makeup?

They were conservative Christians and believed that there was something about the devil that caused you to dress in this manner. Whether devil or angel, you never talked back but just acknowledged their concern and continued with confidence wearing makeup and clothes that pleased you.

I decided then that I wanted to be just like you – to have a mind of my own and to wear beautiful clothing. "It might happen," I thought.

Even if not, I could still dream.

The Guess Place
We had the Music

Dear Alma,

You were always listening to the radio no matter where we lived. In the houses with no electricity, you listened to a battery radio. Those batteries must have been powerful as the radio stayed on all day - you listened to it constantly.

From morning to evening, country music filled our house.

You and I sang right along with Patsy Cline as she sang "Walkin' After Midnight"… or with Hank Williams as he crooned "Hey Good Lookin'". I really liked those songs. I thought they were about you. Everyone knew you were good looking. I couldn't help wondering, though, where you went after midnight.

I liked many of the other country music songs of the 1950's but didn't understand them. When Ernest Tubb declared "I'm Walking the Floor Over You", I'd wonder whose floor he was singing about and if someone was buried under it.

Two of your favorite songs were "Lovesick Blues" and "The Wild Side of Life". You were neither sick nor blue and I didn't know what the wild side of life was. Maybe it had something to do with wild animals.

Jim sometimes thought of himself as a wild thing but he wasn't an animal. Clearly, as a 5 or 6 year-old child, I didn't have a clue about the meaning of the lyrics of these songs. But, I liked words, rhyme and rhythm and I really liked listening to the music just like you.

As an adult, I think that a constant diet of the country music from the 1950's must have had an influence upon teenage listeners and perhaps given them a warped sense of relationships.

For you, though, I like to think that it was just entertainment, offering a break in your world of poverty and work. And, I still like country music.

The Guess Place
A Test of Wills

Dear Nora,

I have mostly vague memories of you while we lived on the Guess Place. You were a little baby who cried a lot, especially if Mom wasn't holding you. Charles and I thought you were getting way too much attention.

Daddy worked at a gas station in Shively. I remember his working nights and trying to sleep during the day. The sleeping was difficult with a baby around – especially as Mom started to wean you. So, to provide a quiet house for Daddy, Mom would take you to the barn.

I can almost see her as she was then, carrying you in her arms and then sitting in an old straight back chair in the barn rocking back and forth.

She would milk a small amount of warm milk directly from our cow and try to get you to take it from a bottle or a cup. I believe she thought that since the milk was fresh and warm, it would seem like breast milk to you.

But you weren't easily fooled. It took a few weeks and other tricks before you were weaned. Once, Mom even blackened her breasts with soot from the fireplace thinking you would be frightened and not want to nurse any more. When that didn't work, the struggle to wean you continued.

It mostly became a contest of wills – yours against Mom's. Eventually Mom won. She decided that if you were hungry or thirsty enough, you'd take whatever she offered. She just had to be firm enough to endure your crying.

You did finally decide to drink from a cup. Charles and I didn't understand exactly what was going on. We thought you were just a spoiled little baby trying to get all of Mom's attention. You seemed to have taken over the center of our universe and we didn't much care for it.

Soon our universe changed again. We moved to the Grimes Place.

The Grimes Place

We moved to the Grimes Place when I was 6.

The Grimes Place was on Springfield Road, less than a mile from the Guess Place. Again, we were just renters.

The house was a mansion compared to the house on the Guess Place. It was the largest in which we had lived.

It was a frame house covered with brown "rolled siding" (a siding popular in the 50's) that was supposed to resemble brick. We always referred to it as brick siding.

The house had four spacious rooms downstairs and two smaller rooms upstairs. My siblings and I thought we were "movin' on up". We still didn't have indoor plumbing but we did have electricity. It seemed miraculous to me that I could flip a switch on the wall and light would flood the room.

The Grimes Place had other attractions. There was a large pond where a snapping turtle lived, pastures and a barn for livestock, a large tree by the road perfect for hanging a rope swing and even a grape arbor in the back yard.

Me, in the front yard of the Grimes Place.

Alma, and I would stand under the arbor and eat grapes until we burped them back up. Best of all was what the Grimes Place didn't have. It didn't have a muddy lane where cars were constantly getting hung up.

As was typical, we only lived at the Grimes Place for a short time, about a year. Still, it was long enough for many adventures and misadventures. I was old enough to run around outside with my brother, Charles, who was nine. He and I continued to cement our relationship over resentment at all the attention Nora was getting. Alma was working at restaurants in Elizabethtown where she met Ernest Pearson, a soldier whom she later married.

For the first time, an outsider became a part of our family.

The Grimes Place Panther on the Prowl!

Dear Alma,

When we lived on the Grimes Place in 1951, you had already started working in Elizabethtown at The Food Basket, a popular restaurant.

When you were home during the day, you continued to listen to the radio non-stop. In the evening after supper, you listened to serial radio dramas. I especially remember your favorite broadcast, "The Black Panther."

In this drama, the plot was always the same. A black panther was loose and stalking neighborhoods. He could not be caught. Each time the panther was spotted, someone would notify the sheriff. But, before the sheriff and his posse arrived, the panther managed to slip away. Night after night the hunt continued.

I was six years old - not old enough nor experienced enough to understand the difference between fact and fiction. I believed whatever any adult told me and believed that anything I heard on the radio was real. The cry of the panther and the terror in the voices of people in the neighborhoods sure sounded believable to me. I was torn between wanting to listen and wanting to hide. I'd listen for a while and then go into another room. But then, I was afraid I'd miss something. I'd return asking, "Have they caught him yet?" "Not yet," you'd answer. "Maybe tomorrow night."

Mom tended to be over protective of me so I'm surprised she let me stay in the room and listen to the broadcast. But I continued to listen every time you turned it on. And, I continued to be both curious and afraid.

Each evening, as the black panther stalked neighborhoods on the radio, in my mind he was stalking just outside our door. Eventually, either the serial ended or you became too bored or too busy to listen. I didn't know what happened to the panther but I was relieved. He must have been captured or wasn't stalking any more. I relaxed and forgot about him for a while, at least in my waking hours.

For years afterwards, though, a black panther stalked me in my dreams.

The Grimes Place
A New Adventure

Dear Alma,

Do you remember this picture?

I'm sitting on a horse outside the big tent of a traveling circus in Elizabethtown, Kentucky, The year is 1951. The horse isn't real of course. It is like one you might see on a merry-go-round.

I am smiling and holding the reins of the horse that also appears to be smiling. I am wearing a western style hat. The horse has a similar hat, hanging from leather straps held in his mouth. I am wearing a dress with a Peter Pan collar and short puffed sleeves. It is the dress I was supposed to wear on the first day of school.

You are standing beside me. You have shiny long dark hair hanging down your back. You have your arm around me and you are smiling. You are wearing a dress in a style similar to mine with a Peter Pan collar and short sleeves. I'm sure you bought this dress yourself.

You were working at The Food Basket, a popular Elizabethtown restaurant, and were earning your own money. You had started buying clothes, jewelry and makeup for yourself and little surprises and gifts for me and for other family members.

You have a black handbag, or as it was called then, a pocketbook, draped over one arm and you are holding cotton candy in your hand. You have the other arm draped around me. People who didn't know us must have thought that we were mother and daughter.

"I can't believe this day really happened I think to myself." It was weeks in the planning. First, when you asked Mom if you could take me to the circus, she said "no".

Mom was an unsophisticated, country woman who never had time or money to travel or to participate in what she considered "frivolous" activities. She tended to be a bit leery of the unknown and also tended to be over protective.

She was worried about the kinds of people we might encounter at a circus as well as what germs or diseases might be floating around. She also knew that she had no money to buy tickets. But, over several days, you wore Mom down and told her that you had money for the tickets since you were earning your own money now.

Alma and me at the circus.

One by one, you answered all her objections.

So early in the morning of this summer day, we arose early. I was shivering with excitement and could hardly wait to get into the car and be on our way. As we drove to Elizabethtown, I kept bouncing around and asking questions until you threatened to take me back home.

Finally, we were there. You pulled the car onto the dusty, dirty grounds of the circus. There were no paved parking lots as there would be today - just patches of asphalt and gravel where the tents were set up and where parking space was provided for visitors. This was only a temporary headquarters for the circus. In a few days, it would pack up and leave town on a train heading for other places.

What A Day!

What a day we had! First we toured the areas outside the tents where sideshows promised glimpses of bearded ladies and two headed men, or of a sheep with 5 legs and other such oddities. Scurrying right on by, we made our way to the Big Top, the tent where the main acts were held.

The Ringmaster's voice rang out as he strutted around in his brightly colored coat and top hat. Twirling a cane, he pranced around the ring announcing each act.

I loved the beautiful horses with fanciful and scantily

dressed ladies riding bareback. I loved the elephants, especially the baby elephant that hooked his trunk onto his mother's tail and followed her everywhere.

The clowns were fun, too. I watched sad clown, Grumpy, with teardrops painted on his face and his partner, Happy, with a large red nose and a huge smile painted in red. Giggling with the rest of the crowd, I jumped up and down and clapped my hands as Happy turned flips, fell down, taunted Grumpy, and finally coaxed a smile from him.

The tight-rope dancers were entertaining but kind of scary. They danced across a tightly strung wire high in the air. The audience gasped as the dancers faked a fall just to add excitement.

Then came the trapeze artists! As they jumped from a platform and flew through the air, I could barely breathe. Putting my hands over my face, I squinted through my fingers and peeked through just enough to catch a glimpse of these daring performers. When their act was over, I let out a big sigh of relief. Already, though, I was hoping to see them again.

"Wasn't that fun?" you asked as you took my hand and led me out of the main tent. "You looked a little scared," you said.

"No, I wasn't scared," I replied. "My eyes were tired and I had to close them a little bit."

Once outside the tent, we walked the perimeter where we saw caged lions and tigers and other animals. Then, we followed our ears and found a merry-go-round.

I quickly picked out a horse. After helping me up, you stood beside me as we rode around and around listening to the calliope. I was getting tired but didn't want to admit it. Nodding, my chin dropped to my chest and I jerked it back up.

When the music stopped, we left the merry-go-round and walked some more. You spotted a vendor where you bought lemonade and an amazing pink treat that looked like cotton on a stick. I couldn't imagine what it was. When I tasted the pink cotton, like magic, it melted to a sweet liquid on my tongue. Later, wiping my sticky hands and face as we were getting into our car, you asked, "Sissy, how did you like your cotton candy?"

"Ah, so that's what it was," I said. "Thank you. I loved it."

As we left the parking area and headed toward home, I felt like I was saying good-bye to a fairy tale. I was tired and quickly fell asleep. When we arrived home, it was almost dark. Mom was waiting anxiously for us. I woke just enough to walk into the house.

"I'm glad you're back," Mom said. "Did you have a good day?" Then she led me to the living room sofa where I fell back to sleep and became a star in my own circus.

The ringmaster steps to the center of the ring. "Look this way folks! Look this way. Here's Jean and her beautiful companion Fancy." I enter the ring, dressed like a princess, riding bareback on a beautiful horse…

The Grimes Place
Skipping School

Dear Hubert,

Wow! It had been a busy week.

We had been talking about and planning for me to start to school in 1951 when I was 6. During the past week, I received more attention than I had at any time since Nora was born. Alma cut and styled my shoulder length hair with perfectly even bangs in front and curls all around. Mom purchased a new dress for me – a pretty dress made from plaid gingham with a little double collar of white organza. Mom usually made our clothes so I knew this dress was special. Going to school must be very special.

A couple of times I had been to school and spent the day in the classroom with you.

Although that probably wouldn't be allowed now, it wasn't so unusual in 1951. Especially on picture day, many older students brought their younger siblings to school to

1950 & 1951 visiting school on picture day. I didn't start school until 1952 when I was seven.

have their picture made. So, I was ready. I had a new dress and haircut. I was experienced from spending time in my brother's classroom. How hard could school be? I was anxious to find out.

But, maybe I was just fooling myself. When that big yellow bus showed up on the first scheduled day of school, I decided I wasn't ready to start after all. Hiding my face in Mom's skirt, I cried and held onto her. I didn't want to get on the bus. Compulsory school enrollment age was 7 years old. So, rather than make me go, Mom let me stay home.

Consequently, I didn't start school until the next year.

That additional year at home was special to me. Nora and I were the only children left at home during the day. Nora was only 2 and napped often. You and Charles were in school. Alma and Jim were already working.

So this year with Mom was almost like it used to be before Nora was born. I matured and became more secure in my place in the family. By the time school started in 1952, I really was ready to go.

The Grimes Place Measles

Dear Charles,

When we moved to the Grimes Place, you and I continued to be best buds. Hubert was five years older than you, already a teenager. You and I were closer in age. I turned six and you turned nine while we lived there. I was supposed to start to school but then cried and Mom let me stay home.

During that year you caught the measles at school and brought them home to me. By the way, did I ever say "Thank You?"

Neither of us had a severe case. We ran a slight fever and felt bad for a couple of days. But, we continued to play and hardly slowed down. Then, Nora caught them and you would have thought she was dying. She cried and cried and cried. We thought she was just being a baby and crying to get attention. After all, the measles hadn't bothered us that much.

She soon recovered from the measles and then refused to learn to walk. While Mom's other children had started walking at or before 12 months, Nora did not. She was going on two and still not walking.

Mom and Dad were worried and thought they might have to take her to the doctor to be checked out. You and I, of course, thought this was just another of her tactics to remain a baby and to get all the attention.

When she did finally start walking at 18 months, we kind of wished she had not. We didn't much like having her toddle along behind us everywhere we went.

The Grimes Place
City Cousins

Dear Charles,

Remember how we didn't know many of our kin folk other than our immediate family?

Our aunts, uncles and cousins were spread out all over the country. Grandma and Grandpa Hawkins died years before we were born. Grandma and Grandpa Sego were getting old. They lived in Glendale with Uncle Tom and Aunt Sarilda. We did meet the Butlers or the "city cousins" as Nora used to call them.

Remember Aunt Ermine, and Uncle Willie Butler? Aunt Ermine was Mom's youngest sister. She and Uncle Willie lived in Louisville. Like us, they had a large family.

One night after Mom and Daddy were notified that Grandpa Sego was very sick, the Butlers showed up at our house. Aunt Ermine and Uncle Willie left Coneta and Freeman, their two youngest children, at our house while they went to Glendale with Mom and Daddy.

"What strange names," I thought. I had never heard them before. Coneta was about your age and Freeman was just a little bit younger than me. Hubert was left in charge.

What a time we had that evening. We ran through the house like, as Mom would say, "a bunch of wild Indians."

We played tag and hide-'n'-seek. You took the fun a little too far when you hid under the stairs and jumped out at me as I went by. I screamed with fright and to this day I am easily startled.

Worn out by all the excitement and playing, we decided to go to bed – or at least upstairs to the bedrooms. There, we used the mattresses as trampolines and the pillows as weapons. Feathers flew as we pounded each other in one of the biggest pillow fights ever. Mom and Daddy would have "skinned our hides" if they had been at home.

Finally, we did settle down and fall asleep. The next morning we awoke to the news that Grandpa Sego had died.

The Grimes Place
Other Relatives

Dear Charles,

We met a few of our other relatives while living at the Grimes Place.

Thomas Hatfield, our cousin, spent a lot of time at our house while we lived there. He had a job in Elizabethtown, as a taxi driver, I believe. He boarded with us to be nearer his job. His parents, Aunt Ida (Daddy's sister) and Uncle Omar (her husband) lived in Hart County near Cub Run.

Having another "almost adult" in our household was a good thing. When one of the biggest snow falls of the century came in the winter of 1951-1952, Thomas helped Jim to dig out and go get groceries. Thomas and Jim had many good times together.

Uncle Ben, Daddy's oldest brother, and his wife, Aunt Edith, also came to visit while we lived on the Grimes Place. I kind of remember showing them the hen house

Nora and me in the chicken pen.

and our baby chicks. In one picture I have of them, they are standing in front of our house with Mom and Daddy as they get ready to leave and go back home to Big Clifty.

Uncle Ben and Aunt Edith came to visit.

We spent more time visiting Uncle Ben later on. His oldest daughter had married Forrest Duvall. She and her family lived just across the road from Uncle Ben. Do you remember all the Duvall children, our second cousins? I thought they were rich. I loved going to their house to play. One of their bedrooms had connecting closets; you could go in one closet and out the other. I thought this was the greatest thing I'd ever seen. Patsy Duvall and I played together in these closets.

Life was good for me while we lived at the Grimes Place. Daddy was away from the house a lot.

He worked in Louisville – most of the time at a Spur gas station. Each day or night when he went to work, he took lunch with him in a big black lunch box. When he got home after work, I would always try to meet him and carry his lunchbox to the house. Daddy got a kick out of leaving me a treat. Sometimes it would be a piece of a fried pie that Mom had sent with him. Occasionally it would be a candy bar.

You and I continued to be best buds. We spent our days swinging in the tree by the road or playing near the pond where we always watched for the snapping turtle that lived there. Daddy always said he was going to catch the turtle and make turtle soup. He never did, though.

We stopped thinking so much about Nora soaking up all of Mom's love. Daddy worked steadily and could afford to bring us a treat now and then.

I got a new "store bought" dress to wear when I started school but then didn't have to start to school after all.

The Grimes Place Puppy

Dear Charles,

We had lots of fun on the Grimes Place but life wasn't all fun.

I remember when our neighbors down the road had a litter of new puppies and promised to give you one when they were old enough to leave their mother. You were so excited at the prospect of having your own dog that you picked out the puppy you wanted and visited him every afternoon. By the time he was old enough to leave the litter, you were already attached. But, you hadn't given him a name. You and I just referred to him as Puppy – not "a puppy" or "the puppy" – just Puppy as if that were a proper name.

Mom and Daddy had always had farm dogs that lived outside and never came into the house. They reluctantly agreed to let you bring Puppy home but said that he would have to live outside.

Well, a few days before he was to come home to our house, you started to prepare. You fashioned a makeshift dog house out of an old crate that you found in the barn. You brought it out and placed it near the house under a tree. Mom gave you a couple of old towels and you placed them inside the crate. You scrounged through some junk in the barn and found a bowl to use for water. You were ready.

Finally the day arrived and you brought Puppy home. We played with him in the backyard, petting and talking to him until almost dark. Then you put him in his house and we went inside ours. Early the next morning you rushed out to check on Puppy. Instead of finding him in his house, you found him near our back door, sleeping on the ground.

"This won't do," you thought. "This is the middle of winter." You tried to talk Mom into letting you bring Puppy inside but she wouldn't agree. So, you put him back into his house and petted him, telling him he would have to stay there. You went off to school as usual.

By the time you arrived home from school that afternoon, snow had started to fall. You checked on Puppy and gave him fresh water and food.

Before bedtime, you sneaked one of your old flannel

shirts outside and wrapped it around Puppy. You hoped that the shirt would keep him warm and that your smell on the shirt would keep him happy. As we prepared for bed that night, the snow continued to fall. Mom predicted that school would be called off for the next day. "Oh boy," you said. "I'll get to spend more time with Puppy."

Mom was right. The snow continued to pile up overnight.

When we got up the next morning we looked out the window and saw a deep snow with even deeper drifts here and there throughout the yard. You hurriedly dressed and pulled on some boots and a jacket then dashed out the kitchen door.

When you didn't return after several minutes, Mom stepped outside to look for you. She found you sitting in the snow, cradling Puppy in your arms and crying.

Puppy had come out of his shelter during the night and become trapped in the snow. He had frozen to death.

The Grimes Place
Just a Truckin'

Dear Jim,

Do you remember that old flatbed truck we had when we lived on the Grimes Place? There were side racks that could be attached, but most of the time they were left off. You liked to drive that truck around the fields near our house.

One afternoon, when you and Hubert were finished with the chores, you decided to have a good time with the truck. Just about then, Charles and I walked back toward the barn to play. You and Hubert climbed into the cab of the truck and told Charles and me to hop on the back.

The side racks were not attached, so there was not much to hold on to. We scooted close to the cab and found openings where the rack would have fit. Sticking our fingers into these, we held on as best we could.

Everything went well until you wanted more

excitement. You took one lap around our pond at a leisurely pace and then sped up like you were driving in the Indy 500. About that time, I lost my hold and went sliding off the truck bed. Landing on a grassy spot near the pond, I rolled over and stopped just before rolling into the water.

You didn't even know that you'd lost me until Charles started banging on the back window of the cab. Then you stopped and ran straight to me. You picked me up and brushed me off. "Are you hurt?" you asked. "I don't think so," I said in a quivering voice. Then you sat me in the cab with you to ride back to the barn.

Later, as we all walked to the house, my arm started aching. I looked at it and there was no visible injury. Just then that old cat of ours came along and started rubbing against my ankles. Remember that old cat? He was always getting his tail caught in the screen door. I didn't like the cat very much and I really didn't like him rubbing against me. I'd kick him away and he'd come right back. Anyway, shortly after we all got back to the house, we went inside. No one mentioned our mishap with the truck. A little later I started to go out again. My wrist hurt badly as I pushed open the door and then I started to cry.

"What's wrong? Why are you crying, Sissy?" Mom asked. Well, that old cat must have still been on my mind. "Because the cat got his tail caught in the door," I answered.

Mom surely didn't believe that but she didn't question me anymore. I don't know why I was afraid to tell Mom that I was hurting. This wasn't the first or last time I was unable to tell her that I hurt.

Soon after this incident, we moved again.

This time to Ford Highway.

Ford Highway
Road with No Name

Whenever I think of growing up, I always think of Ford Highway. We lived on a small farm of about 25 acres located on Ford Highway in Hardin County Kentucky. Ford Highway was not really a highway.

When we moved there it was only a graveled country road located about six miles from Elizabethtown, running between Valley Creek Road and Middle Creek Road.

From one end to the other was about three miles. Because it was narrow and unpaved, school buses didn't come down the road. To catch the school bus, students had to go to the intersection either at Valley Creek Road or at Middle Creek Road.

As Hubert told it, the road didn't actually have a name when we moved there. Daddy wanted to get the road taken over by the state and widened so that the school bus would come out that road to pick up children in front of their own homes. This would mean an increase in property taxes. To have it taken over, a petition had to be signed by all the property owners along the road.

The Ford family lived in the last house on the road and Mr. Ford didn't want to sign the petition. He was the last holdout.

Daddy spoke with him several times but had no success in getting him to sign it. Eventually, Daddy became so frustrated that he, as a joke, posted a hand painted sign with the words Ford Highway at the intersection of the gravel road and Valley Creek Road. I'm not sure why, but after the sign was put up, Mr. Ford soon signed the petition. The state took over the road, improved it and posted an official street sign: Ford Highway. The name has remained through the years.

We lived on Ford Highway during the early 1950's for almost five years – longer than at any other place before or after. It was an ideal place for children. Crime was practically non-existent. Neighbors knew and looked out for each other.

Most attended Valley Creek Baptist Church, the same Baptist Church that we attended. The small farm on which we lived was a natural playground for kids and teens.

Ford Highway
I Think They Like You

Dear Charles,

Remember all the fun we had on Ford Highway?

Our backyard didn't have a play set purchased from Sears Roebuck or some hardware store. Our play set was free, supplied by Mother Nature. We had trees where we hung a rope swing. We had stumps left when other trees were cut down. We ran and climbed and jumped over these stumps when it was dry weather. When it rained, we had puddles in which to splash. We didn't even know about the kinds of play sets found in the back yards of many children today.

We didn't need a swimming pool. We had our own pond in which I played and you swam – I never did learn to swim. It was hard to swim in a dress and I wasn't allowed to wear shorts or slacks.

We played in that pond for the entire summer after

Daddy had it dug. Then, the next summer I came out of the pond one day with leeches on my leg. You pulled them off and told me that they were blood sucking parasites. "What's that mean?" I asked. "Leeches live on human blood and if they find a human they like, they'll hang on and keep sucking until the blood is all gone. I think they like you," you said.

Later in the summer, I started feeling sick and my skin turned yellow. I thought for sure that you were right and those leeches had sucked all my blood. Mom and Daddy never did take me to the doctor. They just said that I had "the jaundice."

As an adult I discovered through a blood test that I had contracted Hepatitis A at some time in the past. Thinking back, I knew it must have been that summer. I probably caught it from the pond water.

After I had the jaundice, we abandoned the pond as a swimming pool. We found other ways to have fun, though. We didn't need playground equipment like sliding boards and swings. Our back field was full of red sandy gullies created by erosion. Sliding down those gullies was way more fun than sliding down a sliding board.

A rope swing hung from the big oak tree in our yard let us soar as high as we dared. And, the woods beside our house were full of wild grape vines – perfect for swinging.

While we lived on Ford Highway, you and I continued to be best buddies. We spent most of our time together when we weren't doing chores.

Nora was three when we moved there - not old enough to go out and romp in the woods and fields with us. By the time we moved away, she was almost seven.

She could walk with me to the mailbox out by Valley Creek Road. She could play with me in the areas close to the house where Mom could watch us. We'd lie in the grass and look at the clouds finding those that looked like animals. We'd search the grass for 4-leaf clovers convinced that when we found one, we'd really have good luck. We'd try to figure out a way to reach the end of a rainbow and lay claim to a pot of gold.

The days on Ford Highway were close to perfection for country kids like us.

Ford Highway
Mr. Sherrard's Bus

Dear Hubert,

On a typical autumn morning in September of 1952, I climbed aboard a big yellow bus to begin the adventure of a lifetime.

You and Charles were with me and were very protective. I was a little nervous but knew that you would keep me safe. I had ridden the bus one time before when we lived on the Grimes Place and you took me to school with you to have my picture taken.

Now, I really was starting school and was excited as we climbed aboard. There were no other children on the bus when Mr. Sherrard, the bus driver, stopped for us. He smiled and said hello and then told us to take any seat we wanted. I took a seat in the front near a window. Charles sat beside me and you sat behind me.

As the bus bumped over gravel roads and made stops

at other houses, it began to fill with children. Most were excited to see their friends and to be heading back to school after a long summer.

The bus ride quickly became routine – nothing to dread or fear. Mr. Sherrard was a father figure. He liked kids and didn't mind their talking, laughing, or singing on the bus.

The next stop after our house was the Kings' house where twin teen-aged girls boarded the bus. They were pretty and talented. Every morning they sang - usually religious songs. I particularly remember one: "Life is like a mountain railroad with an engineer that's brave; we must make the run successful from the cradle to the grave…." The analogy between a train and life continued for several verses.

I was too young to understand the message but I liked listening to the girls sing and harmonize. I'd picture a train going up a long hill and wonder if it was going to make it. Soon, I learned the words and sang along.

Now, I understand the analogy. I still love the song.

Ford Highway
Don't Cut My Ears Off

Dear Hubert,

I believe you were in 8th grade when I started to school.

Anyway, you were supposed to watch out for me, take me to my classroom, help me to find the correct bus to ride home in the afternoon, and generally just be available if I needed anything. It didn't take me long to settle into a routine. Handling the classroom was easy. I loved the teachers, the structure, and the classroom activities. I excelled in all academic areas but especially loved reading. I began consuming books.

Handling the playground was a bit more difficult. Each day we had recess when we were allowed to go outside and play. The time wasn't structured and we weren't closely supervised though we were told to stay in specific areas. Big children from the higher grades had recess at the same time as younger kids.

Up until I started to school, my social interactions had been limited to family and a few church friends. I was shy about approaching other children and didn't know how to respond when they approached me. You would always look me up during recess to be sure I was making friends and that I was okay.

Seeing you on the playground always made me happy. That is, until a friend of yours, David, learned how shy and sensitive I was and started to torment me every day. When you found me on the playground, David would always be by your side. He would come up to me and twist my ear and tell me he was going to cut it off. I knew that you wouldn't let that happen but what if he found me when you weren't around? I didn't want to think of what might happen then.

You didn't understand how frightened I was and you knew that David would not hurt me. But, after I complained a few times at home, you stopped coming around me when David was with you. At times though, even when you weren't with him he would find me. I never saw David's knife and don't even know for sure that he had one. I do know though, that I spent half of 1st grade being afraid every time we went out for recess. I was sure David would find me and literally cut my ears off.

Ford Highway
Bully on the Bus

Dear Charles,

Mr. Sherrard continued as our bus driver for the next four years. On most days, everything went smoothly. But, one boy liked to make trouble. I can't remember his first name so we'll just call him Dawson.

Dawson was a bully. He especially liked picking on little girls. Mr. Sherrard scolded him many times but his behavior didn't change. One afternoon when I was in 4th grade and Nora was in 1st grade, as we got on the bus to go home, Dawson took the seat behind Nora and me. He had been pestering us for days and you had warned him to leave us alone. So, on this day, Nora had several papers she had completed at school. She was excited as she showed them to me and talked about showing them to Mom.

Then Dawson reached across the seat, snatched the papers from her and threw them out the bus window. You were furious. You wanted to fight Dawson right there on the bus but restrained yourself as Mr. Sherrard caught your eye and shook his head. Our house was the next stop.

As soon as the bus stopped and the door opened, you jumped off and picked up a piece of 2 x 4 lying there in the grass. You yelled at Dawson and called him a few names, all expletives, followed by cowherd. You dared him to get off the bus and pick on someone his own size. Mr. Sherrard lingered just for a moment and told Dawson to go ahead and get off. Of course, though, Dawson didn't attempt to get off nor would Mr. Sherrard have really allowed it. Instead he closed the bus door and continued down the road.

You stood there in the middle of our lane cursing. Then you calmed down and we went on to the house. For the rest of the school year, Nora and I were frightened that you would really get into a fight with Dawson and maybe even kill him.

But, the school principal dealt with Dawson and assigned him the seat directly behind Mr. Sherrard. Nora and I sat farther back in the bus. For the remainder of the school year, you gave Dawson taunting looks that said, "I dare you to come near my sisters." Dawson must have been so frightened at the sight of a wild boy swinging a 2 x 4 that he didn't tempt fate. We rode out the rest of the year without incident.

Ford Highway
First Love

Dear Alma,

In 1952, I fell in love with school when I started 1st grade at Lincoln Trail Elementary. As you know, our house wasn't filled with books, paper and writing supplies.

The only books we had at home were a Bible, a well worn Children's Book of Bible Stories that had belonged to Grandpa Sego, an outdated copy of the Farmer's Almanac and a Webster's Dictionary. In spite of this scarcity of books, paper and pencils, you taught me the alphabet and started me on numbers. I could recognize a few words. I was school ready and from the first day, I loved it.

Ms. Rhea Kennedy, my first grade teacher, was a very special lady. She visited our home in the summer before school started just to introduce herself. I can't imagine today's teachers doing that. She had a warm and friendly smile. When Hubert took me to the first grade classroom door on my first day of school, I was excited to see that my teacher was the nice, friendly lady who visited us over the summer. Some of the students apparently didn't share my feelings. As I listened to sobs from frightened students and watched them cling to their parents, I wondered, "What is the problem here? Let's just get this class started."

Ms. Kennedy was tall. She had silvery white hair cut into a fashionable style, short and wavy with loose curls. Her hair wasn't blue like that of many older women in the 50's; it wasn't dingy gray with yellow streaks that I had seen on some of our neighbors; it was natural and attractive. Ms. Kennedy smelled like White Shoulders, a perfume you used to wear. I immediately felt safe with her.

The first few days of school were fun for me. For the first time ever, I got to know and play with many children other than Charles and Nora. My fellow students and I got to know Ms. Kennedy. We followed her movements as she came in the door or walked the aisles with the smell of her perfume wafting by.

And she did walk the aisles, rarely sitting at her desk while we were in the classroom. She went from student to student, carefully observing the work being done. "You're doing well, Gary," she'd say to one student. "I like the way you're making your letters," she'd say to another. Pausing beside another desk she'd take a pencil in hand and demonstrate to Susie how to write her name. She had a way of making each student feel cared for and special.

Ford Highway
You Didn't Tell Me About Cheating...

Dear Alma,

You prepared me well for school. I thought I knew everything I needed to know but there was one thing you hadn't taught me – the difference between sharing and cheating.

I was at the top of my class from the beginning. Taking spelling tests was one of my favorite things to do. I always scored 100 and was happy to share my work with those around me who hadn't quite mastered the art of spelling.

When the cute little red haired boy who sat across the aisle looked at me in confusion, I would hold my paper so that he could see it. One day Ms. Kennedy observed me being "helpful" and called me out into the hall to have a chat. I can still feel the heat rising in my face when she explained to me that "sharing" in this way was actually "cheating" and that I should not do it again.

"I didn't know," I said, almost in tears. "I thought I was just being helpful." But, after that, I carefully covered my answers on spelling tests.

As days passed and our class learned other skills in reading and in math, we were soon separated into different groups: the Blue Birds and the Red Birds. It was not apparent to us that we were grouped according to our perceived ability. We thought it was just to make it easier for each student to receive attention. I was frequently assigned as a leader of my group and would assist other students when they stumbled over words or needed help. This, I discovered, was not cheating.

Frequently, I was asked to return graded papers to the other students. I felt proud and happy as I walked up and down the aisles, listening to the sound of my own footsteps and hearing the buzz of other students as they looked at their papers. I was always really glad when that cute little red-haired boy made a good grade.

What is it about cute red-haired boys, anyway? In second grade there was another cute boy with red hair and freckles. I claimed him as my boyfriend for the entire year. I could never say no to red heads and they seemed to always be around and get me in trouble – even the little red-haired boy I ended up marrying.

Ford Highway
Free Lunch

Dear Charles,

"Have I left anyone out?" Ms. Kennedy always asked after reading off the names of the children who had turned in lunch money.

Were you ever embarrassed about not having money? If you were, we never talked about it. You must have gone to school on many days as I did – without lunch or money. You didn't care as much as I did about what other people thought so maybe you weren't as easily embarrassed as I.

Every morning in first grade, Ms. Kennedy collected lunch money from those children who had not brought a packed lunch. After collecting the money, she counted it and then called out the names she had recorded as each child gave her money. The cost of lunch was only a quarter but most of the time, I didn't have that. I sometimes took lunch from home but many times did not.

Daddy told us to ask for a free lunch if we didn't have the money. But, for whatever reason, I was a very proud child. I didn't want other children to know that I had neither lunch nor money. So, when Ms. Kennedy called out names and asked if she had left anyone out, I always raised my hand even if I had not turned in money. She quietly wrote my name on the list for lunch and never questioned why she missed my name so frequently. It wasn't until many years later that I understood - Ms. Kennedy paid for my lunch herself throughout most of first grade.

Many years later, I also discovered that I wasn't the only "special" student in Ms. Kennedy's class.

In 2012, at a high school reunion, I was looking over a roster of attendees and recognized the name of Gary S, who had been one of my first grade classmates. "This can't be the same Gary," I thought. But it was. We soon began sharing memories.

"Do you remember Ms. Kennedy?" I asked.

"She was the best teacher I ever had," said Gary smiling at the memories.

"Yes," I agreed. "She paid for my lunch for an entire year and never embarrassed me in front of the other students. She always complimented me on my work and made me feel important. She never ever raised her voice."

"I remember," Gary replied. "I was shy and afraid when I started school. Ms. Kennedy let me sit on her lap as she read stories to the class. It always made me feel safe."

As Gary and I compared memories, we realized that we had each thought we were the most special student in class. But it wasn't just Gary and me. We realized that to Ms. Kennedy, all students were special. Somehow, in a magical way, she made each of us feel singled out and important.

My first year of school passed quickly but that did not end my connection to Ms. Kennedy. Throughout the next three years, I often saw her talking to my 2nd, 3rd, and 4th grade teachers and became aware that she was "checking up" on me. I knew that I had a friend.

My experience with Ms. Kennedy and other teachers strongly influenced the teacher I became. I can only hope that I nurtured self-esteem and a love of learning like Ms. Kennedy did. She was a very special person.

Ford Highway
The Teacher is Missing

Ms. Kennedy will always remain my favorite teacher. But, Miss Verde Lee White comes in as a strong contender. Miss White had never been married. She clearly loved children even though she didn't have any of her own. She was interesting and independent.

One morning Miss White didn't show up for school. Neither the principal nor any of the other teachers had heard from her. Everyone was concerned and worried. Where could she be? She lived alone. Could she be sick or worse and no one knew about it? Upon investigation, it was finally determined that Ms. White had gone out of state to an educational convention. The only problem was, she neglected to notify her principal or the school board. Within a week, she was back in our 2nd grade classroom.

One of the first things I remember Ms. White teaching us was to discriminate between Standard English and the English spoken by many of our parents.

In her class we learned to say isn't instead of ain't;

threw instead of throwed; learned instead of learnt...

But, all the time she was teaching us Standard English, Miss White taught us to respect the language spoken in our homes – the language of uneducated country people. We were not to go home and tell our parents or siblings that they didn't know how to speak or that they were speaking wrong. We were never to make fun of nor put down anyone because of the language he or she spoke.

I think Ms. White was already 70 years old; it was rumored that the school board wanted her to retire. But she was devoted to education and wasn't ready to give it up. Her students were the better for it.

Ford Highway
What is a Kumquat?

Dear Nora,

We moved before you started 2nd grade so you missed having Miss White for a teacher. You would have liked her. I don't know if there was a standard curriculum guide for 2nd grade. If so, Ms. White didn't let it dictate content nor her method of teaching. She found unconventional methods and unusual topics. Because of that, she made learning interesting and fun.

I will always remember the day she taught us about the Kumquat.

The dictionary definition of Kumquat is: *"an edible fruit; a small oval orange fruit, related to citrus fruits, with sweet skin and tart flesh, eaten whole or preserved."*

I doubt that any 2nd grade student could understand or remember that. Perhaps some of us in the classroom could learn to spell and say Kumquat. Perhaps some could even memorize the definition. But, none of us could have truly known a kumquat until Miss White found a way to make the learning real.

One day, Miss White told us that we were going to learn about a new food. She sat a large jar of fruit on her desk. Then she asked, "How many of you like peaches? How about oranges? How are peaches and oranges alike? How are they different?

After a brief discussion, we all decided that peaches and oranges were alike because they were both fruits and they both had a similar color. We agreed that they both had peels but the peels were different. Then Miss White explained that the peach is a common fruit often grown in Kentucky. "Do oranges grow in Kentucky?" She asked. "No." We all answered in unison. "Does anyone know where oranges grow?" "Some oranges grow in Florida," one student replied. "Yes." Miss White replied. "Many oranges do grow in Florida. I have a fruit in this jar that is very much like an orange. Would any of you like to taste it?"

Some students were reluctant but others were eager. After passing out napkins, one to each child, Miss White opened the jar on her desk and walked up and down the aisles putting a small piece of fruit on each student's napkin. She told students to smell the fruit on their desk. Then she asked for someone to taste it.

Gradually, student by student became brave enough

to try it. "Yuk!" said some students. "Yummy!" said others.

Next, Miss White asked, "Is this fruit more like an orange or a peach?" "An orange," the whole class responded. "You're right." Miss White said. An orange is a citrus fruit and so is a kumquat." Then she took a bag out of her desk and asked, "How many of you would like to take home a kumquat to show to your parents?" She pulled fresh kumquats from the bag and passed them out – one to each student.

I'm not sure how the remainder of the class went. I am sure, though, that I and most of the other students went home excited, eager to show and tell our parents about a new fruit. We were also excited about coming back to school the next day.

Learning was fun in Miss White's class.

Ford Highway
Anywhere a Mouse Can Go

Dear Nora,

You would have liked the unique ways Miss White used when she taught – even topics that could be boring.

When she taught us the parts of speech like noun, verb, preposition, and others, nouns and verbs were pretty easy to understand. But how could we understand and recognize prepositions?

"Easy," said Miss White. "Think of a preposition as anywhere a mouse can go. Prepositions are words like: in, on, out, over, under. Any where a mouse can go." We'd practice being mice and she would call out a word. If the word were a preposition, we'd have to demonstrate – maybe go <u>under</u> the table in front; come <u>out</u> from under the table, even stand or sit <u>on</u> the table. Soon, most students in the class could identify when a word was a preposition.

When Miss White taught spelling, she gave us hints to help us remember difficult words. She told us to always remember there is a <u>rat</u> in separate. Even now, I never wonder whether separate has an e or an a after the p. I just remember a rat.

Miss White challenged the class with more and more difficult or longer words. But, she always gave us clues and helped us break words into syllables. I was so proud when I learned to spell chrysanthemum. It was the longest word I had learned at that time. I would just think (chrys an' the mum).

I was always good at spelling but Miss White helped crown me "queen". We had spelling bees almost every day and I almost always won.

Clearly, Miss White was a gifted teacher who understood and cared for children. She used active and hands-on-learning to teach both simple and difficult concepts. Today's teachers could learn a lot from her.

Ford Highway
We Can Fly!

Dear Charles,

The day we decided to fly was a beautiful summer day. On the small farm where we lived, an old school bus had been converted into a storage building - fodder for a child's imagination. I'm not sure whose idea it was but on this day, you and I looked at each other and at the bus and decided it would be a perfect runway from which to test our flying skills.

Together we built up the idea with more than enough imagination to convince ourselves that we really could fly. We had watched birds glide through the air with seemingly little effort. We had watched chickens flap their wings and laboriously lift into the air. Surely if birds and chickens could fly then so could we.

As we contemplated who would go first and how we would go about it, I could almost taste the sense of freedom that flying would bring. I could feel the air brushing over my face and tossing my hair. I could sense what it would be like to gaze at the sky as I soared upward and then dived back toward earth.

We built up the idea so completely that we never thought of failure. After a brief discussion, we decided you would go first. You were the oldest, largest, and strongest. You would test the air and then hoist me into position and I would go second.

Without hesitation or doubt, you climbed onto the top of the bus. With arms stretched out like wings you began to flap with all your might. Alas, you didn't lift off. It was as if your feet were anchored to the bus. Thinking that perhaps you were too heavy, we decided that I should try. I, after all, was so petite that if a strong wind came along, it could lift me off my feet and into the air.

Perhaps I could lift myself if I concentrated hard enough and flapped my arms just right. I was wearing a dress with wide sleeves so that should help. The sleeves might act like wings.

So my turn came. You helped me up onto the top of the bus. With all the confidence I could muster, I began to flap my arms. The sleeves of my dress ballooned out but I wasn't able to lift off. We knew we would have to do more research to figure out how to fly.

Since we were already on top of the bus, we continued

to try different ways of moving our arms – both arms at the same time, alternating arms, moving our arms faster, then slower. Nothing worked.

What a sight we must have been. Two skinny country kids standing on top of an old bus flapping their arms. Mom came out into the yard and saw us. "Get down from there before you break your neck," she called to us. You jumped off the bus and then I climbed down.

A few weeks after school started back, my teacher read the class a story from Greek Mythology about Icarus. Icarus was a boy whose father, Daedelus, made wings from branches and wax so that the two of them could escape the Labyrinth of King Minos. Daedelus warned Icarus not to fly too close to the sun. But, Icarus loved flying and went higher and higher. He went too close to the sun and the wax melted. Icarus plunged into the sea and drowned.

When I told you the story, you said, "I guess Mom was right. If God had wanted us to fly, he would have given us wings."

But, I wasn't ready to give up on flying. "God had nothing to do with it," I thought. "Someday I will fly."

Ford Highway
Magic Beans

Dear Nora,

I don't think I ever told you this tale from 2nd grade. I know you will get a kick out of it.

Miss White read aloud to us each day after lunch. I mostly loved this reading time. But, not so much on some days. You see, Miss White always let a student choose the story to be read for the day. Each day, I'd hold my breath until the story was chosen.

There were so many stories to choose from like "Snow White and the Seven Dwarfs", "Cinderella", "The Tortoise and the Hare", "Three Little Pigs" as well as many others. The girls usually chose "Snow White" or "Cinderella" and sometimes "Little Red Riding Hood". My favorite was "Cinderella". Every little girl dreamed of being turned into a princess and wearing golden slippers.

But, when it was the boys' turn to choose, they most often chose "Jack and the Beanstalk". This certainly was not my favorite. It disappointed me when Jack seemingly made a foolish decision to trade his family's cow for a few beans. I didn't believe in magic. "Foolish, Jack," I thought.

But, the beans did turn out to be magic after all and grew into a tall bean plant reaching to the sky. One day Jack climbed the bean plant all the way up to a land where a grumpy giant lived. The giant didn't want Jack there and would come after him. Each day, as Miss White began the story, I got very scared. When the giant showed up with his stomp, stomp, stomp, I would try not to listen. But, Miss White read very dramatically and after the first couple of stomps, she would lower her voice as she imitated the giant's voice "Fe, Fi, Fo, Fum," she would declare, "I smell the blood of an English man."

I was sure the giant was going to catch and kill Jack. Every day, when she came to this part, I raised my hand and asked to go to the bathroom. Even though it was just after our lunch break and I had already gone to the bathroom, Miss White never questioned me; she always let me go. I lingered in the bathroom until I was sure the giant had either killed Jack or that Jack had gotten away.

I was an intelligent student who liked good stories. But, I don't think I ever overcame my fear of this particular story. I was at least a teenager or maybe even an adult before I heard the ending. Even today, when I think of it, I suddenly need to go to the bathroom.

Ford Highway
A Real Treat

Dear Daddy,

Sometimes it feels as though I spent my entire childhood on Ford Highway. The years there were certainly my happiest years. I remember more experiences from there than many children have in a lifetime. Like, the first time I learned anything about politics and voting.

The year was 1952. It was Election Day. For weeks I listened to you talking about the presidential candidates. The country was at war with Korea. Both Jim and Ernest had been called up to serve. Jim was in Okinawa and Ernest in Korea.

You were fervent about your support for General Dwight Eisenhower for president. He was running on the Republican ticket and was opposed by Adlai Stevenson, Governor of Illinois, on the Democratic ticket.

General Eisenhower promised that if he were elected, he would end the war in Korea and bring the troops home. I was only seven and had no knowledge of politics or elections.

But, my excitement built for weeks as you talked about Eisenhower. If he was your candidate, then he would be mine also.

Tuesday, November 4, dawned cold and cloudy. I awoke excited. Today I was going to stay home from school and go with you and Mom to Cub Run in Hart County where you would vote.

The drive to Cub Run took about an hour. Nora and I rode in the back seat napping, occasionally hearing you and Mom talk. The mood was serious as you instructed Mom as to how she should vote – a straight Republican ticket. Mom, not politically inclined, would do as most women from her generation did and vote exactly as she was told. Shortly after arriving at the voting site, you and Mom both cast your ballots and we were soon heading back toward home.

The mood in the car was festive. It was as though you knew Eisenhower had won the election. You were cheerful and feeling generous. As we approached Elizabethtown, you asked, "Does anyone want a treat?" Then, you stopped and bought us all an ice cream cone. As we drove on home, I felt special. Getting to spend time with you and to listen to you talk about important things made me happy.

By the time we arrived home, the weather had deteriorated. It was colder and looked as if it might snow.

You polished up the pipes to the wood heating stove and built the first fire of the season. We huddled around it to get warm. I snuggled under a quilt on the couch and drifted off to sleep dreaming about presidents and ice cream cones, hoping your candidate had won.

Then came the waiting. It took hours, if not days, for poll workers to count the votes and report the results. Televisions were not yet common in most households. There were no instant results from the polls and no hourly updates on the radio. My mood vacillated. I'd feel happy and secure that our candidate had won. Then, I'd worry. What if he didn't win? Would that mean the war would never end? What would happen to Jim and Ernest?

I'm not sure when the election results were learned. But, I clearly remember how happy you were. You came home from work and taught me a ditty:

"Ike's in the White House, he's been elected. Stephenson's in the garbage can, waiting to be collected."

I promptly learned the ditty and began chanting it to my classmates at school until I received a reprimand from my teacher. I didn't understand why. After all, my Daddy taught it to me.

During the ensuing years, you continued to vote: 1956, a second vote for President Eisenhower; 1960, for Richard Nixon; 1964 for Barry Goldwater.

I don't know how much you studied the issues but I know that you always voted a straight Republican ticket.

When I turned 18 and registered to vote, I also registered Republican. Later I switched to Independent and then to Democrat. I'm not sure what you would think about that. Would you be disappointed? I don't think so.

Even though we might have some heated discussions, I think you'd be proud that I developed an independent mind. Through your example you taught me that voting is a right and responsibility.

The election of 1952 was a significant milestone in my life. I think about it often and never miss a chance to go to the polls and vote.

Ford Highway
You Were There for Me!

Dear Daddy,

I remember 4th grade at Lincoln Trail Elementary. You worked the 2nd shift at the American Tobacco Company so you never went to any of the PTA meetings or evening programs. You were always at work. Except one time - you skipped work and DID go to school. I'm sure you remember that.

Part of the school's Fall Festival activities was to crown a Prince and Princess. I was running for Princess. Candidates had to collect money and the girl who collected the most would win the contest and be crowned princess.

You were always proud of me and the grades I made in school. For weeks before the Fall Festival, you took my report card with you to work to show it off and to ask your co-workers to vote for me by contributing money. At home, everyone saved their pennies for me. I collected from our neighbors and from friends at church.

Though I didn't know whether I would win, I would

Here I am. All dressed up like a princess!

still be on stage for the ceremony and needed a special dress to wear. Since I didn't have one and we really couldn't afford a new dress, Mom borrowed one from a family in our church. It was a long, pretty dress that made me feel special.

When the evening of the Fall Festival arrived, I was very excited. I couldn't wait to put on my special dress and wear it to school for everyone to admire. I was even more excited because you were so determined that I would win. You took off work for the day and went to see me "crowned."

When we arrived at school, you and Mom settled in the cafeteria where all assemblies were held because the school didn't have an auditorium. Cans on tables in the front of the room were labeled with individual candidate's names. There was mine, clearly labeled. You noticed that people were still adding money to cans for their candidates. I'm sure you didn't have much money with you, but, you emptied your wallet and pockets and put all your money in the can labeled with my name. You were determined that I would win.

I wanted to win that night, more for you than for me. But, another little girl won; I was not nearly as disappointed as you. I felt sad but happy both at the same time.

You were there for me! When I think of that night now, I see a proud daddy showing off a report card to his friends and stuffing money in a can labeled with my name. That was one of the happiest days of my childhood. You were there for me!

Ford Highway
"I Don't Know" Means Yes

Dear Nora,

Do you remember my friend Doris? In the fourth grade, she invited me to go home with her from school and spend the night. I wanted to go but was afraid to ask Daddy for his permission.

So, since you were the baby and seemed to be Daddy's pet, I talked you into asking Daddy for me. You could charm him into anything. Just before supper you asked him. Then, you reported back to me. "He said 'I don't know'." you told me. "But 'I don't know' means yes." you said. You were used to getting almost anything you wanted from Daddy and had learned his language.

I was nervous and excited about going home with Doris. This would be the first time I had spent time away from home without any of my family. But, I really wanted to go.

So, the next day, instead of riding the school bus back to our house, I rode the bus to Doris's house. Immediately, I

**SCHOOL DAYS 1952-53
LINCOLN TRAIL**

The face that could charm the world!

saw that her house was different. It was bigger and prettier than our house. It sat in the center of a pretty, well tended yard. A plaque on the front door said, "Welcome." But, we didn't go in through the front door. I guess it was for important visitors. We went around to the back and entered through the kitchen door.

Doris introduced me to her mother who was friendly and kind. She told me to make myself at home. "Go into Doris's room and put away your things," she said. I can't even remember if I took any extra clothes or if I had anything to put away. But we went into Doris's room for her to change into play clothes.

"What? She has a room of her own?" I thought. We only had two bedrooms in our house. One was for Mom and Daddy. But, when Alma and Ernest lived with us, Mom gave up that bedroom and she and Daddy slept on a bed in the living room. Hubert, Charles, you, and I shared the other bedroom.

Sometimes there weren't enough beds for all of us. We might sleep on a couch or on a pallet on the floor. Until I saw Doris's house, this didn't seem odd to me at all.

After Doris changed into play clothes, I got the biggest surprise of all. She showed me the bathroom. It was in the house! Luckily I was used to the bathrooms at school. Otherwise, I might not have known how to use this one. We still went to an outside toilet at home and we still carried water from a spring. Doris had both water and a bathroom.

Doris and I sat around in her room for a while, talking and telling jokes. Then we went back into her kitchen. A basket of bananas was sitting on the table. Doris told me that her father worked at a grocery store and that he often brought home bananas that were becoming overly ripe. They didn't cost him anything. "Did you have to work there to get these bananas?" I wondered. I made a mental note to tell Daddy about these free bananas. Maybe he, too, could stop by that store and get some.

Then, I met Doris's brother, Jerry. Unlike Charles who always played with me, Jerry went off by himself. A few years later, I heard that Jerry had drowned in an accident at Rough River Lake. That made me really sad for Doris and her family. I remembered how polite and nice he was. I couldn't imagine how much the family missed him. Charles was about his age and if Charles died, I think I would want to die, also.

When Doris's dad arrived home from work, we were called to supper. Everyone gathered around the kitchen table. I noticed pretty dishes that matched – not the hodgepodge that we had at home. Doris's father said grace and then we passed food around the table "family" style. I don't remember everything we were served but I do remember a banana pudding. The pudding must have been made from a mix. It was good, but not as good as Mom's homemade banana pudding.

Meal time at our table at home was more fun than it was at their house. Doris's parents and brother were quiet and talked politely about their day. At our supper table at home, we talked and joked and sometimes even argued over who got the last chicken leg or last biscuit. I could see that Doris' family had more money and a nicer house than ours. But, I wouldn't trade my family for hers.

A few weeks later, Doris came to my house to spend

the night. Her first impression couldn't have been positive. I wonder what she thought as we walked down our lane between a tobacco field and corn field. What did she think when she saw our yard? It wasn't as green and lush as her yard. Like most country yards, ours had spotty grass with mostly wild weeds that the boys kept mowed. But, it did have a row of zinnias that Mom carefully tended. When I took Doris into the house, she looked around and said, "Your living room needs to be painted." Strange, I had never before noticed.

Doris must have been really surprised later when I told her I didn't have a room of my own and that we had an outhouse instead of an indoor bathroom.

She took it all in and didn't complain. We talked and played and then slept on a quilt on the floor. For the first time, though, I began to feel our poverty - to feel somehow "less than" most of my classmates.

That feeling continued to haunt me and spurred me to study hard and work hard to accomplish "respect" among my peers. I didn't want anyone else to ever tell me, "Your living room needs to be painted."

Ford Highway Dolls for Christmas!

Dear Alma,

You were always like a mother to me. You taught me the alphabet and started me reading. You cut and styled my hair. When I was seven, Ernest was in the army and you were getting an allotment check as part of his military pay. You lived with us while he was overseas so you helped with the finances for groceries and other needs. And, you bought Nora and me dolls for Christmas! We had never had real dolls before.

Do you remember those dolls? I think Mom wanted you to buy us baby dolls. But you chose dolls that looked like older children. Mine was dressed in pink. She had a pink dress and bonnet. She had shoes and little white lacy anklets. Her eyes opened and closed. She had a red smile and white teeth.

Those dolls were important in many ways. Nora and I didn't really play with them as much as we just took pride in having them. They gave us each something to own and

Nora and me with our Christmas dolls.

to argue over when we'd trade them back and forth.

Neither Nora nor I could make up our mind about which doll was the prettiest. I'd play with mine a while and then talk Nora into trading. After a little while, she'd want to trade back. Invariably, we would start arguing. Mom got so tired of hearing us argue that she threatened to take the dolls away. Then, we'd be quiet for a while. We didn't want her to take the dolls. They gave us the assurance that when other children came back to school after Christmas with their stories of gifts and toys, we'd also have a story to tell.

I still have my doll although she's beat up a bit now and doesn't have her original clothing. Somewhere along the way, she lost her hair and front teeth. I believe Nora pushed her teeth out but I don't know what happened to her hair.

I still think of her as beautiful, though, because of what she represents. Each time I see her, I think of you and remember what a special sister you were.

The doll is resting comfortably in my cedar chest and will one day be passed down to your great granddaughter.

Ford Highway Pudding for the Preacher

Dear Nora,

Do you remember how Sunday Dinner used to be a big deal? We had dinner in the middle of the day and supper at night.

When we were going to church at Valley Creek, the church had an itinerant preacher, Brother Ray. Brother Ray lived in Leitchfield, more than an hour's drive from Valley Creek. So, on Sundays when he came to preach, he stayed in the community for the day. The preacher ate dinner with a family from church; then, after lunch, he went out to visit other church members.

It seemed to me that he was at our house more than at any other. I believe Mom and Daddy were responsible for finding a place for him to eat dinner. When no other family invited him to have dinner at their house, Mom always asked him to come to ours. Of course, he didn't mind coming to ours; Mom was one of the best cooks around.

Usually, when the preacher was coming, I'd have to help Mom fix dinner. I don't think you helped much. You were still young. You did set the table, though.

We almost always had fried chicken, mashed potatoes, various vegetables, biscuits and banana pudding. It was my job to "make" the pudding. Mom supervised of course. But I had to do the stirring. I stood at that stove and stirred and stirred until my arm felt like it couldn't stir any longer. Mom made me keep stirring, though, until the pudding thickened. Then, in a large dish, I layered either vanilla wafers or graham crackers with the cooked pudding. When I finished this part, Mom made meringue and spread it on the pudding. Then, she put the entire thing under the broiler to brown. That was some of the best banana pudding I've ever tasted.

I rarely make banana pudding now. It's just easier to use instant pudding or to go out to eat. No matter who makes it or where I get it, the banana pudding we eat today never tastes as good as that made by Mom and me in the tiny, hot kitchen of our house on Ford Highway.

All that stirring must have made it special.

Ford Highway
Who Hides a Television?

Dear Nora,

Do you remember our neighbors on Ford Highway? I'll always remember the Nichols family. Our property adjoined their farm and their family and ours became close friends. You were about three when we moved there and I was seven. But, even though I was just a child, I have vivid memories of Ethel.

I will never forget her wedding and how you were supposed to be her flower girl; but, you were too shy to walk down the aisle. She didn't mind, though. She had a beautiful wedding anyway while you sat on Mom's lap and watched.

Do you remember when the Nichols family bought the first television in the neighborhood? Some folks in our small conservative church didn't approve of television. Nellie, Ethel's mother, was really worried about what the preacher would think if he knew they had a television in the house. I can almost hear the conversation she had with Mom. "What am I going to do?" she asked. "The preacher is coming to our house for dinner on Sunday. Should we move the television into a bedroom? Should I cover it up with a quilt or something?"

After much discussion, Nellie decided to leave the television in plain view in the living room and to suffer the consequences whatever they might be. I'm not sure what happened when the preacher came but evidently nothing serious.

Perhaps they spent Sunday afternoon watching "The Little Rascals" or some other popular television show. The preacher didn't run off without his dinner and everyone in the Nichols' household survived. They, along with the preacher, showed up at church that evening.

Ford Highway
A Trip Back

Dear Alma,

Recently, Roger and I took a drive out to Valley Creek Road and Ford Highway. Many things have changed since the late 1950's when we lived there. I almost didn't recognize the place.

But the people have remained the same - warm, friendly and ready to help. We first stopped by Valley Creek Baptist Church and talked with a gentleman who was there to pick up his grandson after basketball practice in the church gym. "My goodness," I thought, this is nothing like the small church I remember."

As we talked, I asked if any of the Nichols' family still lived on the family farm. "Oh, yes!" he said. "Ethel and Pete still live there."

"Could you tell us exactly how to get there?" I asked. "Things have changed so much, I may not remember."

Well, he not only told us how to get there but said, "Follow me. I'll be happy to show you."

Within minutes, we were driving down the lane to Ethel's house. I was just a young girl, but I still remember when Ethel and Pete got married. Her parents worried because he was from out of state, somewhere up north, and even worse, he was a Catholic.

But, Ethel and Pete did get married. They had a beautiful wedding and you were Ethel's Maid of Honor. Ethel's parents needn't have worried. She and Pete have had a long and happy life together.

When we drove up the lane to the Nichols' house, Ethel wasn't at home. But just as we started to back out, she and Pete pulled up. She probably wondered, "who are these people?" when she saw a van in her drive that she didn't recognize. After I opened the van's window and introduced myself, Ethel was very gracious and invited me into her house. We sat on the sofa and talked a bit. Then she said, "Excuse me just a minute."

She soon returned with a picture album. We looked at pictures of her wedding and the two of you together. While we sipped a glass of tea and continued to remember the good times on Ford Highway, Roger stayed outside and got to know Pete. It felt perfectly normal to be there talking.

Thinking of it now, I'm not sure I would have been as trusting or gracious as she. We could have been thieves or murderers.

Ford Highway
You're in the Army Now

Dear Jim,

When you were drafted into the U.S. Army in the early 1950's, Mom and Dad were concerned and worried. They had personal knowledge of what could happen to young men who went into the Army.

Aunt Ida's son, our cousin Roy, had been drafted during World War II. He went missing in action and never returned home. The day you left for basic training was a very sad day. Mom always prayed for her children and had faith that her prayers would be answered. She prayed for you every day.

Our country was involved in the Korean War. You were a young, naïve country boy who had not traveled any farther than Indiana or Tennessee from our home state of Kentucky.

After basic training at Fort Knox, you were shipped to Okinawa where you saw things you never imagined. Although you didn't have to fight on the battle field, you must have had to fight with your previous indoctrinations about people who were different than you. People who had different colored skin or different shaped eyes. People who didn't speak English. People who ate strange foods not at all like the fried potatoes or the beans and cornbread you ate at almost every meal when you were home.

In the small world from which you came there was a lot of "sameness." Everyone looked the same dressed in their work clothes in the tobacco field. They looked the same in the Baptist Church we attended. They ate dinner in the middle of the day and supper at night. In that small world, based on ignorance and lack of exposure to different ways of living, many people, including our family, were prejudiced against the unfamiliar. Sameness was comfortable.

However, when you were in Okinawa, you made friends with local children and found that they were just like the children back home. Although they looked different and spoke a different language, they loved to run and play. They looked up to you and other soldiers as heroes. They loved the sweet treats – candy or gum – that you frequently gave them.

You gained a larger world vision than you ever would have at home in Kentucky. Many of your beliefs and attitudes changed. Yet, you retained your country boy values, work ethic and love of family.

You were a loving son who wrote home often. You sent Mom many pictures. You liked country music and recorded yourself singing.

For a long time, Mom had the record you made but it became broken or lost in all the moving and changing that Mom and Daddy did. Of course, that was way before the time of social media when, if you post or twitter something, it is preserved forever.

What I'd give to have that record now!

Ford Highway
Spilled Pickles

Dear Jim,

While you were in Okinawa, you made a friend, Floyd, also from Kentucky. Soon Floyd was showing you pictures of his sister, Zorada. Her pretty smile and long dark hair attracted you. Within a few days, you began writing to her. The two of you corresponded for over a year. When you returned to the states, you went to meet her in person and soon brought her home to meet Mom and Daddy.

The first time Zorada came to our house, Mom worked all day cleaning and cooking. She was careful to arrange the kitchen table just so. She even covered it with a rarely used linen like table cloth.

I was excited to meet and make a good impression on this new girl who had become an important part of your life. I helped Mom set the table. She and I cut zinnias for a centerpiece. When you and Zorada arrived, we all liked her immediately. She was a quiet and shy country girl who seemed to fit right in with our family.

Jim Hawkins with Zorada Judd

Then we sat down to eat. Supper went well until you asked me to pass the jar of homemade pickles. As I started to pass it, the jar slipped out of my hand and pickle juice spilled everywhere. I was humiliated. "What will Zorada think of me?" I worried. You and Mom quickly jumped up and removed the table cloth. After the table was dried and order restored, supper resumed as though nothing had happened.

Within a year, you were planning a wedding. Zorada's parents threw a wedding shower at their home near Greensburg, Kentucky. Our entire family went and met Zorada's family. Her sister, Susie, was about my age and we became instant friends. After your marriage, you and Zorada moved to Hodgenville where you lived for several years.

Our entire family loved Zorada. Mom and Daddy treated her like a daughter. Alma and she became good friends. Nora and I adored her and thought of her as a big sister.

We all thought your marriage would last forever. But, after more than twenty years together, you and Zorada divorced. We didn't see Zorada much after that. I never stopped thinking of her as a big sister. She and I still keep in touch.

Ford Highway Running Away

Dear Charles,

"Achoo!" I sneeze even now when I think of the tobacco barn on Ford Highway. Remember that barn? It was located at the top of our lane, not far from the house.

As I remember, it was a large open barn with doors on either end wide enough for wagons to pull through. The barn was loosely sided so that tobacco hung inside could air dry or "cure". Cracks wide enough to let the wind blow through were found here and there along the sides of the barn.

When tobacco was cut, usually sometime in August, Daddy along with Jim and Hubert and a friend or another helper, hauled it to the barn. They hung it, stick by stick, on tier poles where it hung until it was cured and ready to strip. Daddy always wanted to get the tobacco sold in time to have a little money before Christmas; he typically stripped it in November.

I remember how cold it sometimes got and how

Daddy propped shocks of fodder against the cracks of the barn to keep out the cold wind. Even after the tobacco was stripped and shipped, small particles and brown dust remained in the barn. The smell and the sneeze factor never left.

I remember the fields on each side of our lane that led up to the barn. In season, tobacco grew in the field on the right side. Corn or some other crop grew on the left. The lane from the house to the barn wasn't very long- probably about ¼ of a mile or less. During the summer, many times early in the morning, you and I meandered up the lane with our eyes searching the ground looking for dew berries.

The thing I remember most about that lane and that barn are the times I "ran off." Picture a little girl about seven or eight years old, marching alone swinging her arms with head up and back straight. That's what I think of now when I remember those days. I was on a mission to make myself seen and heard. Marching straight up that lane to the barn, I always thought someone would miss me and come looking. But no one ever came – not even you. I always gave my mission up after a while and walked backed to the house.

I can still smell the distinct acrid scent of the barn and feel the tobacco dust tickling my nose. I can feel the scratch of the dried corn leaves as I snuggled down in a fodder shock to keep warm.

Looking back, I think I ran away at times when I felt unloved for whatever reason. Maybe Nora was getting too much attention and I was feeling left out.

Maybe Daddy was yelling at Mom as he often did and I sought an escape. Or, maybe I was just mad! Even now, whenever I feel misunderstood or unappreciated, I still feel like running away.

Ford Highway
Little Green Apples

Dear Nora,

"Just as sure as God made little green apples," I can still hear Uncle Gid say. Uncle Gid was Daddy's youngest living brother but he was already middle aged with a family. I'm sure you remember him.

Anyway, Uncle Gid lived in Jefferson County, in Shively, I believe. He wasn't a bad man but he liked his alcohol. Every so often, he would go on a binge and get thrown in jail. The first person he called was Daddy.

Daddy worked in Jefferson County and sure enough, when he got Gid's call, he went down to the jail and put up bail for his release. Then he brought him to our house to sober up. I know Mom must have hated this. Not that she hated Uncle Gid. Nobody hated him. When he was sober he was fun to be around. He told funny stories. All of them seemed to start or end with his favorite saying.

We might be in the middle of a dry spell in summer and Uncle Gid would say, "Just as sure as God made little green apples, it's going to rain tomorrow." Then he'd tell a story about the hottest, driest summer he had ever seen.

Another time, he might tell a story about a crazy woman that he and Daddy knew in their childhood. "She could wring blood out of a dish towel," he would say. "I'm telling you, just as sure as God made little green apples, that woman was a witch." He told story after story and always kept us entertained.

Living with Daddy, Mom put up with a lot. Uncle Gid must have been one of her most difficult trials. She didn't think that anyone should drink alcohol and certainly not to the point of falling down drunk. She understood that Daddy helped Gid because he was family. And, you never turned your back on family.

When Daddy brought Uncle Gid to our house to sober up, we smelled him even before we saw him. The smell was sickening sweet. It was a smell hard to describe but even harder to forget. Each time Daddy brought Gid to our house, Mom washed his clothes to get rid of the smell.

After he sobered up and cleaned up, Gid was always apologetic and promised not to call from jail again. I'm sure he meant it at the time but he always relapsed and it wouldn't be long until Daddy got another call. Gid was an alcoholic who needed more help that Daddy or Mom was able to give. That's the truth.

Just as sure as God made little green apples.

Ford Highway
Paper Roses

Dear Nora,

Do you remember how excited you and I would become as we waited for "Decoration Day." Decoration Day was what Mom and Dad called it.

Looking back, I realize it was probably Memorial Day or Memorial Day Weekend. It was a day when graves were decorated to honor and remember those who had passed on. Not a sad day by any means. It was a day of remembrance and celebration. A day of reconnecting with relatives and friends. A day of worship and praise.

During the 1950's when we lived on Ford Highway, Decoration Day was one of the highlights of our summer.

For weeks our home was filled with activity and anticipation. Mom cooked and cooked. Alma and I made roses.

To be honest, Alma did most of the making. She'd carefully cut petals of different sizes from crepe paper and show me how to use the scissors blade to curl the edge of each petal and to use my thumbs to cup each one. When sufficient petals of various sizes were cut and formed, she would begin the assembly.

She'd put a flower together starting with small petals in the center, holding them in place on a stiff wire to be used as the stem. She continued to add petals with the larger ones on the outside. Next, she would use a very fine wire to wrap around the base of the petals holding them in place. Then, she'd use strips of green crepe paper to wrap each stem completing a perfect rose.

But, there was one final step. She'd carefully dip each rose in hot paraffin that had been melted in the top of a double boiler, then place each rose on a sheet of waxed paper to dry. After several days of crafting, we gathered the roses we'd made and fashioned them into bouquets and set them aside to wait.

When the anticipated day arrived, Mom and Daddy packed the car with food, flowers and children. Daddy drove down 31W to Munfordville and then over dusty country roads to Little Flock Baptist Church where Grandma and Grandpa Sego were buried.

I don't know how we survived those rides. Between the dust and the smoke from Daddy's cigarettes, I'd almost choke. "How much farther?" we kept asking every few minutes. "Are we almost there?" But, we always survived.

There would be an all day meeting with dinner on the ground. Folks from all over came to decorate graves, listen to preaching in the morning, eat and catch up with old acquaintances at noon and stay through the afternoon for gospel singing.

When we arrived at Little Flock, Mom and Daddy walked through the church cemetery reading headstones and reminiscing. When they came to Grandma and Grandpa Sego's grave, they pulled weeds and tidied up the site. Then with great care, Mom and Alma placed the homemade flowers on the grave securing them as best they could with a pointed stick stuck into the ground.

After tending the gravesite and placing all the flowers, women and children went into the church for worship. Preaching and singing went on for what seemed like a very long time to a child but was probably no more than an hour or two. Some of the men would go inside too. Do you remember how most of the men sat together up in front to the left of the pulpit? Is that what people called "the Amen Corner?" Sometimes Daddy went in but at times he lingered outside talking with other men.

Sometime around noon, the preacher dismissed for

"dinner." Then the men hauled out food packed earlier by the women. The women arranged the food on table cloths or sheets spread out under the trees or on wagons or boards set up on sawhorses.

There'd be lots and lots of fried chicken, sometimes a bit of country ham, and usually some meat loaf. There'd be potato salad and macaroni salad (no one called it pasta salad then). There'd be slaw and always a congealed salad made from lemon or lime gelatin with shredded carrots.

Do you think anyone ever ate that orange and green stuff? I didn't and don't think you did either. But, desserts, now that was the good part. There would be cakes – chocolate, yellow, coconut, and always pineapple upside down cakes made with sliced pineapples on the top and fancied up with a cherry in the center of each slice. There would also be pies – apple, peach, chocolate, lemon meringue. The meringue pies usually had wet crusts because the meringue would get "weepy".

Everyone had lots of fun eating and joking. The men talked about who grew the largest tomatoes or the biggest watermelons. Isn't that always the way with the men – talking about who has the biggest?

The women talked about the food, complimenting each other on the pretty cake or the best pie. Later, they went home and said things like, "Did you see that mess that M. brought? And she called it potato salad." Or if they were feeling generous, they said things like, "Wasn't that a beautiful pineapple cake that M. brought? It was delicious, too. But she'd never give us the recipe."

After the meal, folks gradually wandered back into the church and the singing started. Southern gospel songs filled the air - songs like, "I'll Fly Away", "Will the Circle Be Unbroken" and "Whispering Hope." No formal preaching went on in the afternoon. Between songs, folks got filled with the spirit and "testified." Then, the congregation sang some more.

Eventually, the preacher took the pulpit again and started to bring the service to a close. As the congregation sang "Just As I Am," the preacher invited anyone who wasn't "saved" to come to the front of the church. Those who came forward knelt with others who prayed for them to let Jesus into their hearts.

As the service continued, children fell asleep in the pews, men wandered outside to smoke and talk. Finally, after the last verse of "Just As I Am" was sung, the preacher officially dismissed the service.

Then, men, women and children gathered up any remaining dishes from the meal, cleaned up the site, piled into cars and began the journey home.

Later in the summer, we made roses again to take to Lone Oak Church cemetery, also in Hart County, where Daddy's parents were buried. Although Daddy liked red roses, he really loved yellow ones. So Alma and I always tried to make a few of those to put on the graves of Grand Ma and Grand Pa Hawkins. Except for the location, the day at Lone Oak was a repeat of the one at Little Flock.

Reflecting on Decoration Day later, you and I talked about the many "store bought" wreaths with fancy ribbons that we saw on some graves. Those families must be rich we thought.

We wished that our flowers looked like those. Neither of us was old enough or wise enough to appreciate the love and care that had gone into the making of "Paper Roses".

Ford Highway
Valley Creek Church

When we moved to the house on Ford Highway, Valley Creek Baptist Church became a central part of my life. It was there I attended Sunday School and Church on Sunday Mornings, Prayer Meeting on Wednesday Evenings and Vacation Bible School each summer.

It was during Vacation Bible School in 1954 that I made a profession of faith and adopted the motto: I can do all things through Christ who strengthens me: Philippians 4:13.

We went to Bible School for two weeks each summer. I loved everything about Bible School.

I loved the rituals of lining up and marching in behind the leaders carrying the Christian Flag and the American Flag. I loved the cookies and Kool-Aid we had as refreshments.

I loved story time when we read Bible stories and

Bible School at Valley Creek Baptist Church. About 1954.

talked about their meaning and their relation to our life. I loved the challenge of memorizing scripture assigned each day and of reciting it the following morning.

I loved craft time. I can still remember the belts we crafted one summer. Made of paper strips, cut and folded in a special way, the belts were colorful and strong and could actually be worn.

I loved Bible Drills. The call to battle still echoes through my mind: Attention! Draw Swords! Charge!

It was during these Bible Drills that I learned to quickly locate almost any verse in the Bible. I was a fierce competitor and was frequently the first "soldier" to step forward with my Bible opened to the command verse.

The attention and reinforcement I received during these drills became a huge building block of my self esteem. It didn't matter that I wasn't wearing the newest shoes or fanciest dress. It didn't matter whether my family was the richest or poorest in the neighborhood or whether we walked to church or caught a ride with the neighbors. The only thing that mattered was that I was fast on the draw in the Bible Drills and always accurate.

Along with the teaching and reinforcement from home, the lessons from Sunday School and Bible School were huge building blocks in my character development. One lesson at a time a block was laid. Today mental and spiritual strength, tomorrow loving one's neighbor. Tithing and generosity followed. The lesson of the "widow's mite" taught us that the spirit of giving was more important than the amount we gave.

These character building lessons involved more than just the 10 Commandments, although I did memorize those. But, our leaders helped us to understand and to incorporate them into our lives.

What did "Honor thy father and thy mother" really mean? How could we express that in our daily living. What was envy? How could we avoid envying our neighbors even though they might be richer and live in a larger house? What did it mean when we were instructed, "Though shalt have no other god's before me." Surely we didn't have idols or graven images anywhere in our culture. But we did have people who appeared to worship material things above God. Whether it was money, the biggest house or the fanciest car, they were willing to sacrifice time management, Sunday Service and even family responsibilities and loyalty to obtain them.

My experiences on Ford Highway, especially at Valley Creek Church, helped me to find my way to Jean.

When we moved and I started to a different school, I stopped calling myself Delma Jean. From that point on, although I was still somewhat shy, I started to become more assertive and independent. It would be a long road but I would eventually get there.

Ford Highway
Character of a Church

Dear Nora,

You may not remember what Valley Creek Church was like when we first started going there. You were only three years old or maybe three and a half.

The church was a small white building, typical of many small country churches. The parking area was across the road from the church. There was also an outdoor toilet but I don't remember exactly where it was.

It was the people, though, who made the church. The entire congregation welcomed newcomers. Our family quickly became part of the church. Mom helped out in Bible School and Daddy acted as moderator in the business meetings.

Several people in the church had their own personality and talent. Do you remember Lillian who always sat in the aisle seat on the left side of the church, in the front row? She liked to sing and always sang alto. She could be heard above the rest of the congregation. She also liked to keep everyone in order – especially children.

I will never forget the time she had to get after you and me. The congregation voted to build onto the church and contractors had been working all week to get the new part of the building started. Before Sunday, we had a big rain and when we got to church on Sunday, the grounds were a muddy mess.

Well, I don't know what we were thinking. Not thinking at all, I guess. We were, after all, just little kids.

After church started, you and I had to go outside to the toilet. Then, we loitered around and splashed in the mud. Lillian just about had a fit when we came back into the church tracking mud everywhere. Mom, I'm sure, was totally humiliated. She took us back outside and cleaned off some of the mud. Then we started home. We didn't even go back inside; I don't think Mom could face Lillian any more that day.

Ford Highway
I'll Fly Away

"Shall We Gather at the River," the gathering of about 35 people sang as we came together around the banks of Valley Creek. Voices blended in harmony.

Lillian's voice soared above the rest. Lillian was a tall, gray haired lady with a big voice. She always sat in the aisle seat of the front left row during regular church services. She occupied a no less prominent place here. Under the canopy of trees beside the creek, she stood in the front of the crowd. She didn't want to miss seeing anyone or to have anyone miss seeing her.

Brother Lay, our itinerant preacher, raised his arms and stretched his hands toward the group in a gesture of blessing. His voice rang out, "We are gathered here this morning..." Candidates for baptism lined up with the shortest ones in front. I led the pack.

Although Hubert and Charles swam in the creek (in fact, this was the very spot they had claimed as their swimming hole) I had never been allowed near it. Mom believed that girls and women should wear modest clothing at all times. Modest, in her interpretation, meant no slacks or shorts and certainly no bathing suits. I had never even stuck my toes into a creek or river. I had no idea what to expect as, wearing my best Sunday dress, I stepped gingerly into the edge of the water.

My skirt puffed around me; I felt as if I might float away. Then Brother Lay reached out his hand and led me into the water until it was just above my waist.

"Do you, Delma Jean Hawkins, profess your faith in the Lord Jesus Christ as your savior? Do you come here today to be baptized and express your faith to God and man?"

"I do," I said.

Then, Brother Lay placed one of his hands behind my back and the other over my mouth and nose.

"I baptize you in the name of the Father, the Son and the Holy Spirit," he said, dunking me below the water. Then, as he raised me back up from the water, I felt a strange sense of joy and peace. I wanted to skip around in my happiness. "I'll Fly Away," we often sang. I wondered if this would be the day.

Many of those gathered at the creek were skeptical that a child of nine could experience true conviction and salvation. I only knew that a few weeks before, after a day at Vacation Bible school, I had lain awake one night unable to sleep. Pondering on all I had been hearing all week about Jesus and about asking for the forgiveness of sin, alone in my bed I asked Jesus to come into my heart. On that night, I experienced an immediate relief and sense of peace.

The next morning I wanted to talk about it to Mom but could not. I started to bring it up again and again but would always change the subject to something else – something trivial like going to the watermelon patch to get a melon.

It seems strange now when I realize that I couldn't talk with her about anything important. I think it was because Daddy yelled a lot and Mom looked unhappy much of the time. I learned to "protect" her – never wanting to do anything to add another load to her life.

Anyway, I went off to Bible School that morning as usual. When the invitation was given at the end of the service for anyone to come forward to express their belief in Jesus and their desire to be baptized, I was one of the first to do so. The pastor met with me afterwards and believed I had experienced a genuine spiritual awakening. He spoke with Mom and on Sunday morning I went forward to join the church. Now here I was being baptized.

From that time forward I have considered myself a Christian and have tried to live a life patterned after what I understand of Christ.

The belief and confidence that began in a small Baptist Church on Valley Creek Road and culminated in my baptism in Valley Creek has served me well. My understanding of what "being a Christian" means has changed over time. It has not always been constant but has given me strength and hope.

From the time of my conversion at the age of nine, my motto has been Phillipians 4:13: "I can do all things through Christ who strengthens me."

Ford Highway
Bull in the Berry Patch

Dear Charles,

Do you remember picking blackberries in the fence rows and fields of our neighbors on Ford Highway? We'd head out together, just the two of us, swinging a bucket or carrying a pan. Sometimes Mom would go with us but not always.

One of our neighbors had a large bull in a field where we liked to pick. Mom warned us not to cross that fence and go into that field. But of course, you weren't afraid and you sure wanted those blackberries. You somehow knew or thought you knew that bulls were attracted to the color red. You cooked up a plan that I would stand on the safe side of the fence and wave a red cloth to get the attention of the bull. You would sneak around to the other side and go into the field to pick. It sounded like a good plan. We decided to try it out.

After a few minutes of picking, you had a bucket full

of juicy berries. Then the bull became bored with me and head down in attack mode, turned and ran straight for you. I stood petrified unable even to scream and warn you.

Catching a glimpse of movement out of the corner of your eye, you knew at once what it was. Running toward the fence you knew the bull was about to catch you. You hurled the bucket of berries toward his face to slow him down. Making it to the fence just in time, you scrambled over and forgot about blackberries. I let out a sigh of relief.

When we arrived back at home a little while later with not much to show for our morning of picking Mom wondered, "Where are all the berries?"

"Oh we didn't find many ripe ones today," we said in unison both afraid of what Mom would do if she found out we had disobeyed her.

After a while, though, you couldn't resist telling your version of the story portraying yourself as big and brave and not afraid of any bull. Then you laughed telling everyone how frightened "Sissy" was.

Ford Highway
Last Picking

Dear Charles,

Blackberries were a recurring theme in our life on Ford Highway. I'll never forget the last time we picked them. It was the summer of 1955.

No one cultivated blackberries at that time. They were nature's gift and were found growing in fence rows and uncultivated fields. We didn't have any bushes on our property but all the neighbors allowed us to pick from theirs.

Blackberries were plentiful that summer. So, on our last day of picking, we went out with 2 empty buckets and heads full of hope. We had been watching a particular spot in our neighbor's field. It was grown up with all kinds of wild plants and vines. We avoided it in our earlier pickings because we found the picking easier in the fence rows.

Today though we knew the season was almost over and those vines in the jungle like field were loaded and bending over with fruit. Knowing that this might be the last time we picked for the season, we couldn't resist pushing our way in.

Fighting heavy growth of all kinds of wild plants, small trees, grape vines, and even some poison ivy, we were determined. We finally made our way to the mother lode. We lifted one bent over vine after another and the berries practically dropped themselves into our buckets.

Of course we couldn't resist sampling the product. The berries were so plentiful that we could eat some along the way and still have more than enough to fill our buckets. After an hour or so of picking, we picked our way back toward an open field that led to our house. What a sight we were. Blackberry juice stains on our face. Scratches on our arms and legs. Hair disheveled. Two buckets running over with fruit. And, covered with hitchhikers that we couldn't even see.

We arrived back at the house and I started itching and breaking out with red spots all over my body. The hitchhikers had been chiggers. I was literally covered with them from head to toe.

Mom stripped me down and bathed me in a milk bath. I was so miserable for a few days that I didn't even want to think of berries. Mom continued to bathe me with milk and I finally started to feel better. I promised myself that I would never pick blackberries again. That turned out to be an easy promise to keep. Just as I was itching all over, Daddy had come down with another case of itchy feet.

We soon moved again – to Cecilia, a small town on the other side of the county. No blackberries growing in fields or fence rows there. We were in for different kinds of adventures.

Ford Highway
Sand Gullies & Underwear

Dear Charles,

"Come on, Sissy! I have our Kool-Aid. You bring the peanut butter and crackers," you said as you motioned to me from just outside the kitchen.

I grabbed a paper bag already filled with our lunch and hurried through the door. We were on our way to the natural adventure park behind our house. We could have more than enough fun there without struggling through briars or running from bulls.

At the top of the hill behind our house was a child's paradise created by nature. We loved to play army there. Large craters and sand gullies carved out by erosion made a perfect battle zone. For hours, with stick rifles as guns, we ran, ducked and shot at each other. When we tired of battle, we rested and ate some lunch. Then we played war a little longer.

What funny looking soldiers we must have been with red Kool-Aid mustaches and peanut butter smeared everywhere. We pretended that the peanut butter on our clothes was camouflage.

When we tired of battle for the day, we abandoned it and wandered down the dry creek bed that bordered the field. Eyes peeled to the ground, we searched for fossils and crystals. You, of course, usually found the best fossils. You talked to me about how fossils came to be – how most fossils started out thousands of years ago as live animals. I really didn't want to hear about that, though. It made me kind of sad. I didn't like to think about dying animals. But, I did like searching the dry creek bed with you.

Some days we didn't find any fossils. But, we found pretty crystals and pretended they were diamonds. You told me that the crystals came from sandstones. Sometimes we found large sandstones and took them back to the house where you broke them open.

We found many crystals – enough to line the perimeter of Mom's flower beds. Then, even if the flowers weren't blooming, the bed was kind of pretty with crystals sparkling like diamonds in the sun.

Some days we didn't pack a lunch. We cut our playing short and returned to the house hungry. But, you soon took care of that. You mixed up some biscuit dough and cooked biscuits in Mom's double fry pan. We sliced tomatoes from the garden and made biscuit and tomato sandwiches. That was really good eating.

Mom got upset with us for playing in the sand gullies so much. She said we were ruining all our underwear. And, indeed we were.

After a day of sliding around there, our formerly white underwear would be stained red forever. Mom must not have been too upset, though. She never gave us a "good talking to."

Ford Highway
The Auction

Dear Charles,

One of my most poignant memories of you is the day of the auction when Daddy sold the property on Ford Highway and anything he owned involved with farming – including Barney and Prince – our two work horses.

I knew that you and Hubert really liked those horses but I didn't realize how much you loved them, especially Barney.

Hubert had left home by this time and you had taken over almost as the sole caretaker for the horses. At the end of a workday, you climbed on the back of one horse and took the reins of the other in your hand. You led them to the pond for a long drink before taking them back to the barn and freeing them from all their harness and gear.

Occasionally I rode one of the horses to the pond; but, being a big "sissy" as you called me often just to goad

Hubert riding Barney, our horse.

me into doing whatever you wanted me to do at the moment, I didn't like taking the horses for a drink. When the one I was on bent his head low to get to the water, I was sure I was going to slide right over his head and into the pond.

So, anyway, the big day arrived and we were all excited. It was a sunny day in mid-summer and the atmosphere was humming. It was like a party. People milled around and talked.

The enormity of what was taking place had not sunk in yet with you and me. As the auction proceeded, we played around running from one place to another. Then it was time for the horses to be auctioned. We stood in silence listening as the auctioneer rapidly moved from one bid to another, one bidder to another. When it seemed all the bidding was over, "Sold!" he said to the highest bidder.

Soon a truck backed up to the field by the barn and Barney and Prince were brought out to be loaded onto the truck. It struck you then that this was probably the last time you'd see them. You ran up to Barney, putting your arms around his neck and started crying. I knew you were really upset because you never cried about anything.

Your way of handling sorrow and pain was to strike out in anger. But, you couldn't contain yourself this time and even anger didn't show up to bail you out.

Daddy went up to you and removed your arms from Barney. "You have to let go, son" he said. Barney is going to his new home now.

You took off and ran to the hill behind our house where you and I spent so many happy afternoons playing. Of course, I followed. But you weren't in a playing mood this time. "Leave me alone. Go on back to the house," you sobbed.

What seemed a very long time later, when the sun was going down, you returned to the house. Together we helped with the packing and getting everything ready to move the next morning.

Reality set in and we knew that we were leaving Ford Highway for good. Uncharacteristically, as the sun went down and darkness came, our mood became just as dark. It was as if we knew that the sun would never again shine as brightly on our life.

We were saying goodbye to a part of our childhood. Though I was only ten and you thirteen, our carefree days of roaming the fields were over. We would soon begin an entirely new way of life in the small town of Cecilia.

Cecilia
A Different Way of Life

When I was 11 we moved to Cecilia into a 3 room house at the end of a street and directly across from a propane gas storage facility. Large trucks would come to the storage facility to return empty tanks or to pick up filled tanks to take to customers. Mom didn't like living that close to the storage facility. She feared that an accident would happen and the entire place would blow up.

The house had running water in the kitchen but didn't have an indoor toilet. When nature called, we still had to go outside to the outhouse. The house had a gas range in the kitchen where Mom cooked and it also had electricity.

As soon as we moved there, Daddy bought our first television. Charles and I stayed up late on one of our first nights in this house to watch a movie about Elvis Presley.

Within a few days of moving to Cecilia, we started to meet neighbors. Nora quickly made friends with the family next door who had two daughters, Martha and Libby, about her age. Charles made friends with a boy, Paul, whose family lived at the end of our street. I didn't meet anyone my age but that was fine with me. I could hang out with Charles or Nora and their friends or I could hang out with my books. Books were always my friend.

The move to Cecilia was momentous in many ways. I entered 5th grade at a different school than the one I had attended for my first 4 years. I left behind my beloved First Grade teacher, Ms. Kennedy, who had continued to watch out for me as I progressed through 2nd, 3rd and 4th grades at Lincoln Trail Elementary.

I left behind my best school friends: Donna, Janice and Doris. I left behind the only stability of place I had known, the small farm where we lived for almost five years. I left behind the relaxed life style of rural living where we had neighbors close enough to reach out to when help was needed but far enough away to allow for privacy. I left behind the freedom of roaming the fields and woods beside our house and of going on long walks to the mail box that was approximately a mile down the road.

It wasn't just the things I left behind that caused this to be such a momentous occasion.

Upon moving to Cecilia I was exposed for the first

time to a diverse neighborhood that included a colored (as they were referred to then) family, a Catholic family, and churches other than the Southern Baptist Church we had always attended.

I was exposed to neighbors whose family make up was very different from ours – a family consisting of a father and two daughters. Where was the mother, I wondered. There were other families - one, consisting of a matriarch and her two adult sons or grandsons. We never did know their exact blood relationship. A couple, Ruby Durbin and Hugh Clark, lived on the same lot but in separate houses. Their relationship and housing arrangement is still a mystery to me. I believe that now they would be living together as a couple. But, in the 1950's that would have been looked upon as sinful. Hugh and Ruby regularly got into arguments in the middle of the night and woke all the neighbors as they "chased" each other around the yard yelling obscenities and threatening to shoot each other. Eventually, someone would call the sheriff who would come and calm things down.

My exposure to "Coloreds" and to Catholics – especially Catholics - was a big deal at the time.

Though I didn't realize it, our family was very conservative and quick to form opinions about those who were different from us – especially the Catholics and the

"Colored".

Mom's and Daddy's definition of a "good" family seemed to be - a husband, a wife, children, and membership in a protestant church, preferably Baptist. The husband provided financially for the family and the mother stayed home and reared the children. And, of course, the family was Caucasian. Anyone outside these parameters was looked upon suspiciously.

A Catholic family lived next door to us. This family had two girls, M. and L., about Nora's age. They attended a Catholic school and church within walking distance of our house. Each morning when they left for school or church, they wore a hat. I thought that was strange. We had never worn hats except at Easter. As I got to know these neighbors, I discovered that it was a Catholic ritual for girls and women to wear head coverings in the church.

Since students at the school attended mass every morning, girl students usually wore hats. Sometimes, if they forgot their hat or just didn't want to wear one that day, they would simply put a white handkerchief on their head as they went to Mass.

As I learned more about the Catholic religion, it started to have an appeal to me. Catholics were more traditional. They practiced rituals that were established years ago.

Rituals and consistency appealed to me. They suggested stability and strength. Also, Catholics appeared to have more money and to be better educated than the Baptists I knew. I began to think of Baptist as a "poor man's religion."

The Catholics we met did not hide their beer or wine as I knew some Baptists did. The family who lived next door to us kept beer in their refrigerator. Their church served real wine at communion and sold and consumed beer openly at their annual picnics or their Friday night fish fries. The Catholics I met didn't appear to worry over sinning as Southern Baptists did. They apparently accepted, as a matter of fact, that everyone sinned. So they went to Confession, told their latest sins to the priest, and heard him pronounce, "Your sins are forgiven."

Our Baptist religion also taught that everyone sinned. The biggest sins, as preached from the Baptist pulpit, appeared to be related to sex, money, and alcohol.

Preachers in the Baptist churches preached a "Thou shalt not" religion. Thou shalt not drink alcoholic beverages, thou shalt not steal, thou shalt not kill, thou shalt not get it on with your neighbor's wife. If you did these "bad" things, you would go to hell.

Instead of confessing through a priest, Baptists confessed directly to God. They didn't experience a human voice telling them they were forgiven.

Thus, even after confessing in prayer, Baptists tended to continually worry and to feel guilty. I spent much of my childhood worrying and feeling guilty.

As an adult I came to believe that worrying and feeling guilty are wastes of time and energy. How I wish I had understood that earlier in life.

Cecilia
Thanksgiving Goose

Dear Charles,

Do you remember our first Thanksgiving in Cecilia? Before we moved there, Thanksgiving was much like any other day. We never had a big meal with all the family. We never went "over the river and through the woods" to Grandma's house

The best thing about Thanksgiving was the special free meal served to all the children at school on the day before. That lunch always included turkey and gravy with stuffing and mashed potatoes, cranberry sauce, and green beans. Usually a piece of fruit, maybe an apple or a plum, was included for each child to save and take home for later.

Another good thing about Thanksgiving was a two day break from school. We stayed home and did whatever we wanted.

You always hoped for a tracking snow on that day.

You liked to go rabbit hunting and a light snow made it easier to track rabbits. Mom cooked as usual – maybe a little bit of fried ham at noon to go with the potatoes and beans we always had.

Sometimes she made something extra like a special cake or a chocolate pie. I don't remember ever having pumpkin pie. The only thing we knew about having turkey for Thanksgiving was what we heard from all the stories the teachers read to us and all the paper turkeys we made at school. We never had turkey at home.

Our first Thanksgiving in Cecilia was different.

Two Negro men, Rod and George, who lived down the street, brought us a goose to welcome us to the neighborhood. Rod and George were known and liked in Cecilia and all over that part of the county. Every one called them "N… Rod" or "N… George". I can hardly write it or even think it now, but the "N" word was common then. Anyway, they brought Mom a goose already cleaned and ready to cook.

When Rod and George left, Mom looked at that goose and said, "What am I supposed to do with this thing?" She didn't quite know how to cook it or even if she wanted to. She was a really good cook but not very adventurous. Since the goose looked somewhat like a big chicken, she decided to cook it the same way.

    I don't remember whether she boiled or baked it but I think she made cornbread stuffing like that she made for a baked hen. I do remember that we all thought the goose was one of the best Thanksgiving meals we'd ever had.

Cecilia
Responsibility

Dear Nora,

By the time you were old enough to run around and play, I had already forged a strong sibling bond with Charles.

He and I were a little closer in age than you and I. When we lived on Ford Highway, Charles and I were allowed to roam the hills and woods without adult supervision. You were too young, only three when we moved there, and had to hang around the house with Mom.

Our nieces, Joyce and Judy were born in 1952 and 1954. Alma and the girls lived with us while Ernest was in Korea. When he came home, they were still at our house much of the time. Joyce and Judy became your playmates.

When we moved to Cecilia, you and I still didn't spend much time playing. Martha and Libby lived next door and they were your age. You spent much of your time with them – either at their house or at ours. I spent most of my time hiding away somewhere with a book. Charles and I continued to have more in common than you and I did.

Many of my memories of you are tinged with feelings of responsibility.

Do you remember our first days of going to Howevalley Elementary School? We'd walk together in the mornings to the Cecilia Restaurant where we caught the school bus. I was very careful to hold your hand as we walked and to keep you close by as we waited.

Mornings were not bad but afternoons made me nervous. I was a 5th grader "a big girl now" and was responsible to see that you, a 2nd grader, boarded the correct bus. "What if your teacher let you leave the classroom by yourself before I stopped by to pick you up," I worried. "What if I somehow couldn't find you and you caught the wrong bus? Would we ever find you again?" It wasn't long though until you became confident in finding the bus yourself.

Your teacher and the bus driver got to know you and I began to relax a little. I didn't worry as much but I carried that feeling of responsibility into adulthood.

Cecilia
New Kid on the Block

I always loved school at Lincoln Trail. I thrived on the attention of my teachers and on my success in the classroom. I had good friends who started school the same year I started. We came from similar backgrounds and knew each other well.

School became difficult for a while, though, when I started 5th grade at a different school, Howevalley Elementary. The teachers there didn't know me. Most of the students, even those in the upper grades, had attended the same school together since 1st grade. I was the new kid on the block and not immediately welcomed by other students.

I had a tough time making friends at Howevalley.

One particular student, let's call her Jane, had been at the top of the class since 1st grade. When I came in and gave her competition, she didn't like it very much. I actually didn't even know that, but even if I had, I'm sure my competitive nature would still have emerged. I was proud of my academic ability. On every quiz or test I strived to be the best. If Jane scored 100, I wanted to answer an extra credit question so I could score 105. If Jane received an A on a writing assignment, I wanted an A+. If we had spelling bees, I wanted to be the last student standing. So, Jane's reputation as the smartest child in 5th grade was threatened.

Not long after I enrolled, she started a "Hate Hawkins" club. Yes, bullying was alive and well in 1956. I don't know how many students joined her club. I did learn many years later from a friend of Roger's that he knew about the club as did other students in the 6th grade class.

Mr. Joe Goodman was my teacher in 5th grade. I had never had a male teacher but soon discovered that he was a good teacher who loved children and teaching as much as my previous teachers had. He brought special things to school to share with students as Miss White had done with the Kumquat. The thing I remember most is divinity his wife had made. When I took a piece home and Mom tasted it, she asked for the recipe. She and I continued to make divinity for several years at Christmas Time.

Well, maybe divinity isn't the thing I remember most. What I remember even more is the time I unwittingly got even with Jane.

Mr. Goodman was always teaching vocabulary. One afternoon, we were discussing how words that sound the same may have different meanings. We talked about the word bus as being a noun, a thing that had wheels and usually carried people. A school bus was a good example. "Who knows another way to spell bus?" Mr. Goodman asked. When no one answered he said, "Bus can sometimes be a verb and is spelled buss." I had no idea what this buss meant but when Mr. Goodman asked who knew it, I immediately raised my hand. "Can you show us what it means?" he asked me. "Why don't you buss Jane?" Walking to Jane's desk, I confidently smacked Jane on the side of her face. "No. That's not right," Mr. Goodman said. Buss means to kiss. So I gave Jane a kiss on the cheek and went back to my seat. For the remainder of the day, I smiled to myself. I had slapped my biggest enemy and hadn't been punished for it.

When I enrolled in 5th grade, I took advantage of an opportunity when Mr. Goodman asked me what I wanted to be called. "Jean," I said. I didn't explain to him that my family called me Delma Jean. He introduced me to the class as Jean and I never told the other students my full name.

At the end of the first grading period when I received a report card, it said Jean not Delma Jean. When I took the report card home, Mom and Daddy asked, "Is this your report card?"

"Yes," I answered. I never explained to them that I told Mr. Goodman to call me Jean. They and most of my family continued to call me Delma Jean or Sissy. To myself and others, I was Jean. Jean felt right. I really was the new kid on the block.

The Railroad House Party Line

We didn't live long in the first house we moved to in Cecilia. In less than a year, we had moved to the Railroad House. It was the best house we had lived in up until that time. Situated by the railroad track that ran through Cecilia, it was a pretty white house with a front porch and a swing. The house was spacious with a kitchen, a living room and two real bedrooms. Nora, Charles and I were the only children still living at home.

As she did in every house into which we moved, Mom went right to work turning it into a home. She let me help her pick out wallpaper and then help her to wallpaper the bedrooms. She planted flowers in the yard around the house. Soon, we felt right at home. Mom and I hoped we'd live here for a long time.

The Railroad House had some modern conveniences. We still had to use an outhouse but we had running water in the kitchen and we had electricity. When we flipped a switch, like magic, a light came on. More miraculous than the lights was the phone. I never believed we'd have a phone. But now we did. We were on a "party line," a line shared by neighbors. We could pick up the receiver and, if one of our neighbors happened to be on the line, we could listen to their conversation. No matter how many times Charles and I got into trouble when Mom caught us listening, the temptation was always there. We'd pick up the receiver numerous times during the day and listen.

Charles, ever the prankster, picked up some ideas from friends he'd made at school. He started using the phone for fun. He and his friends would dial the number of a store and ask, "Do you have Prince Albert (a brand of tobacco) in the can?" Without waiting for the answer he'd say, "Well you better let him out before he smothers." Then he'd hang up and laugh along with his friends.

One of the first things I did after moving there was to call my best friend, Donna C., who was still going to Lincoln Trail Elementary. I could hardly wait to let her know where we had moved and to tell her how much I missed her and all the other friends and teachers at Lincoln Trail. We promised to call each other often – to always keep in touch. Unfortunately, we didn't follow up on that promise and have not seen or talked to each other in more than 50 years.

I believe that if we did see each other today, we would pick up the friendship. Years would fall away like days, taking us back to the playground at Lincoln Trail.

The Railroad House
Shooting the Moon

Dear Alma,

Do you remember when we lived in the house by the railroad in Cecilia? We had so much fun there.

You were already married and lived in Elizabethtown with a husband and two little girls, Joyce and Judy. I loved it when every Sunday afternoon your family came to our house. Joyce and Judy played with Nora. Mom cooked and tended to the kids. But you, Ernest, Daddy and I played Rook.

Mom never played cards with us. I think she thought playing cards was sinful. Nevertheless, Daddy loved to play Rook and he needed a partner to form a foursome. So, he taught me. One lesson at a time and one game at a time, I learned the basics. I learned about following suit and counting cards. I learned to bid based on the cards in my hand and to not be afraid to bid for the "kitty." Soon, I was playing as good as most of the adults and I was almost

Daddy as I always remember him

always Daddy's partner.

Do you remember how fearless Daddy was in his bidding and how he hated to lose? Any time our opposing partners were about to win the game, no matter what Daddy held in his hand, he would "shoot the moon."

That meant he and his partner had to catch every trick of that round. If he was successful, he and his partner won the game. If he was unsuccessful, the opponents won.

As his partner, I would concentrate and count cards as they were played. I played carefully and frequently had just the card needed to give Daddy points or to take the trick myself. I really wanted to win. But, win or lose, Daddy's way of bidding and playing made the game exciting and fun.

The Railroad House Popcorn & Soft Drinks

Dear Alma,

I've been thinking about all the Sunday afternoons in Cecilia when you and your family came to visit.

As we played cards we sipped soft drinks and nibbled on popcorn. You and Ernest brought the drinks. Having soft drinks was a really big deal for us kids. We almost never had them. Mom didn't spend money on snacks or drinks. She was frugal with what little money Daddy gave her for groceries.

Do you remember the afternoon we ran out of drinks and wanted more? The Cecilia Restaurant was just across the railroad and about a block down the street from us. The restaurant was open on Sunday afternoons and sometimes we'd go there to get drinks or even ice cream.

One Sunday when we needed replenishments to get us through a tough afternoon of playing Rook, you and I volunteered to walk to the restaurant for more drinks and goodies. But there was a problem. A train depot was located not far from our house. Trains stopped there to get water.

Well, that afternoon a long train had stopped at the depot. It was blocking the road and stretched as far we could see. Sometimes, when a train stopped like this, it seemed like it didn't move for hours.

"What are we going to do? How can we get across the tracks?" I asked. You were clearly Daddy's daughter. As he was fearless when shooting the moon, you were fearless and somewhat reckless when you wanted something. Looking at the train across the track you said, "This train isn't going anywhere. Just follow me."

Then you ducked under one of the train cars. I was too young to think of the danger. But, even if not, I would have followed you anywhere. So, we crawled under the train. After purchasing drinks and ice cream, we headed back home. The train was still blocking our way, so, we once again crawled under a train car and made it safely to the other side. We took our goodies home and were soon snacking and playing Rook again.

As I think of that day now, I understand what a reckless and dangerous thing we did. But danger wasn't on my mind as I followed you under the train. It was even more exciting than Shooting the Moon.

The Railroad House Dancing

Dear Nora,

I'm sure you remember The Cecilia Restaurant better than I. Across the tracks and about a block down from our house, it was a popular hangout in Cecilia It was a perfect place to get a cup of coffee in the morning or a hot meal at noon. Adults liked to hang out there and catch up on neighborhood gossip. Teens liked to meet up with friends there and listen to the juke box.

Remember Mrs. Speck, the owner? She was friendly and outgoing. She welcomed teens there any time. Every school aged child in Cecilia, whether in 1st grade or 12th grade, gathered there each school day morning to wait for the school bus. The older kids played songs on the juke box and danced. I really liked watching the older girls dance and itched to join them. I was only in the 5th grade when we started going there and most of the dancing girls were in High School.

Mom didn't want us to dance. I believe she thought that dancing was a sin.

Once, Grandma Sego stayed in our home for a while. As usual, our radio was constantly on. I felt the music and went around the house bouncing to the rhythm. You could hardly call it dancing. Yet, when Grandma saw me bouncing around, she said in an accusatory voice, "What are they teaching you in that school, anyway?" She must have thought that "they" were teaching me to dance. Of course that wasn't true. I just had the music in me. From that day on, I didn't dance in front of Grandma or Mom. I knew they disapproved.

In the beginning, I also didn't dance while waiting for the school bus at the Cecilia Restaurant. I did, however, observe. By the time I started 7th grade, I was joining in the dancing and the older girls taught me to rock and roll. I still didn't dance at home. As with so many other things, I felt I had to hide it.

What fun it would have been if we could have said, "Look, Mom! Watch us dance." It would have been even more fun if she would have held our hands and danced along with us.

Cecilia
Peter's House

I believe we moved into the Peter's house about the time I started 7th grade. The house was on the same street as our first house in Cecilia. It was just across the street from the backyard of the railroad house. We didn't live in the house very long. It came with an extra lot on which Daddy built a new house.

The Peter's house was a two story house with weathered siding. When I read John Grisham's book, <u>The Unpainted House</u>, I always think of our house on the Guess Place and of the Peter's house in Cecilia. The ceiling of the upstairs in the Peter's house sloped down toward the eaves of the house. Two unfinished rooms - more like an attic – became bedrooms for Charles, Nora and me. Shortly after moving in, Mom went right to work to improve the rooms. She tacked brown cardboard on the unfinished walls and covered them with wallpaper. She hung ruffled curtains at the small window. The transformed "attic" rooms made a perfect getaway for children.

On my bed, tucked away under the eaves, I day dreamed and forgot all my worries.

Here, in the attic, I read for hours without being disturbed. I educated myself about the facts of life. I searched the dictionary for words like "sex" and "pregnant" and read books loaned to me by an older girl in the neighborhood.

Then I took this information with me to school and listened closely as other girls talked. I tried to put it together with the information in the film shown to 6th and 7th grade girls. I never asked questions but finally figured out on my own that I couldn't be pregnant.

When I think of the Peter's house now, I remember the attic room as being one of my favorite rooms ever.

Cecilia
Peter's House

Dear Nora,

You started to become a more important part of my life about the time we moved to the Peter's house.

You and I shared a bed and talked more. We both started school at Stephensburg Elementary – you in the 3rd grade and I in the 6th grade. We attended church at Cecilia Baptist and made lots of friends there.

Do you remember when my BTU class from church was going on a hayride? I wanted to go but didn't have jeans or slacks to wear. Mom said I could go but would just have to wear a skirt. You understood how embarrassing that would be so you asked one of our friends, Debbie C. if I could borrow a pair of jeans?

Did I go to her house and put them on just before going to church to meet others for the hayride? I can't remember for sure. Maybe you brought them home and I managed to sneak away with the jeans under my skirt.

I do remember that when I got home from the hayride, I went to the outhouse in our back yard and took the jeans off. I stashed them in a paper bag until we could give them back to our friend.

As with dancing, I wish I could have talked to Mom about clothes and made her understand how important it was at times to dress to fit the occasion. It was years before I wore slacks or shorts in front of her. In fact, I didn't wear them at all until after I left home and married Roger.

Much of my teenage angst could have been alleviated if only our family had talked more.

Cecilia
Memory from 7th Grade

Mr. H. strutted into the 7th Grade classroom with briefcase in hand. Without a greeting to the students, he opened the briefcase and took out a stack of mimeographed papers. "Here's your surprise test for the day," he said before sitting down at his desk. For the next 30 minutes, as students struggled with the test, Mr. H. sat looking out at the class with a smirk on his face. The smirk was a fixed feature.

Mr. H. is one of the few teachers I look back on with disdain. He was a 30 year old male of average height, slender and effeminate. He had black hair & dark eyes. His slender hands and long fingers looked like those of a pianist. Mr. H. spoke well for someone who had grown up in rural Kentucky. He had perfect diction but a slight tone to his voice that suggested superiority. Mr. H. came from an upper middle class family; he was an only child who had been indulged by his parents. Consequently, he thought of his teacher salary as menial. He must have thought that teaching was beneath him.

Mr. H. was unmarried and never spoke of a

Here I am giving the valedictory speech at my 8th grade graduation.

relationship. It was rumored by some of his students that he "liked" boys.

He grew up in a "holiness" church whose members were conservative and strict. In public, the women wore long skirts and long sleeves with their hair conservatively styled, twisted into a bun at the back of their head. Mr. H. dressed conservatively as well. With a smile to replace the smirk, he would have been an attractive man.

Mr. H. had beautiful penmanship, even when writing on the blackboard. His greatest talent, however, was a talent for making his students feel inferior. I was a confident student, though, and never felt inferior in the classroom. Perhaps Mr. H. resented my confidence; he tried to put me down by telling me, "You'll never amount to anything." If I could see him today, I'd say, "Look at me now. Look how wrong you were!"

Cecilia

Dear Charles,

Once again, I wish you were here to help me refresh my memory. I can remember writing a paper for you when you were in High School. I know that we lived in Cecilia but I can't remember in which house.

You might have been a senior. In that case, we would have been living in the new house that Daddy built beside the Peter's house. Anyway, you needed to write a research paper. The paper was due in a few days and you hadn't started it.

I always liked to write and you thought I wrote well; so, you talked me into writing the paper. You didn't explain that it was a research paper and I didn't know exactly what a research paper was. I didn't know that it required documentation from several sources indicating you had actually researched a topic.

You had chosen or had been assigned the topic of school integration. Not only did I not know what research was, I didn't know anything about integration. But I got right to work. "What does integration mean?" I asked you. I don't think you understood it completely. Both you and I had always gone to schools with other students who looked just like us. We didn't know that some students, just because their skin was a different color, weren't allowed to come to our school.

Your class had obviously held some discussions about integration; you explained that it meant white children and black children could go to the same school.

I was immediately full of questions. "Can't any child who wants to come to our school just ride the bus like we do?" I asked. "Can't they come to our school now?"

"I haven't seen any black kids in our neighborhood. Where do black kids live?"

Question after question popped into my head and out of my mouth. I started taking notes on the answers. Then, when Daddy came home from work, I started asking him about his thoughts on integration.

That discussion was the deepest and most meaningful discussion we ever had. Daddy had talked to me before about politics and elections but I didn't ask questions; I just took what he said as truth. This time, I listened to his opinions but also asked questions and added a thought or two of my own. We had a real discussion with give and take.

I learned that Daddy didn't think black and white children should go to school together. He thought that if they went to school together, black teenagers would start dating white teenagers and he thought that was wrong. He thought schools where black children went then were just fine. I found myself thinking about his answers and not always agreeing.

I wrote a paper for you that night – based on what you had told me about where black children lived and about the schools they attended.

Mostly, I wrote about what Daddy had said. As I was writing, I had even more questions but they would have to wait until another time.

You received a C+ on that paper along with a comment from your teacher. "This is a good paper, but it isn't a research paper. If you had done your research and documented your sources, you might have received an A."

Cecilia
High School

In the fall of 1960 I started high school at Howevalley High. Once again I was thrown in with students who had started first grade there and would stay there through high school.

Their families lived in the surrounding community. Many were even related. I was an outsider.

I would again encounter the girl who had started a "Hate Hawkins" club in 5th grade when I was the new kid on the block and she didn't like being displaced as the top academic student.

None of those things, however, deterred me from being excited. I had been the top student academically in my classes at Stephensburg Elemenary and popular enough to have been elected class president each year in 6th, 7th, and 8th grade. So I plunged into high school with confidence. Soon, I found my place there.

I became 9th grade president, a member of the Beta Club, an officer in the FHA Club, and made enough friends that I didn't have to walk the halls alone nor sit by myself in the cafeteria. I even became friends with Jane who had formed the Hate Hawkins Club when I was in 5th grade.

Within weeks of entering ninth grade, I spotted a boy with dark auburn hair and a shy smile. Yes. Much like in 1st Grade, I was charmed by another red head. He was different from most of the other boys. He dressed neatly and spoke politely. He was one of the popular kids who had gone to Howevalley his entire life.

When I finally got around to asking someone his name, I found out it was Roger. Roger was at the top of his class academically. He was a leader in the FFA club and an officer in his 10th grade class. He played sports – basketball in the fall and baseball in the spring.

With the annual fall festival scheduled in a few weeks I began to tell my new friends that I was going with Roger. They didn't believe me – after all, they had known Roger his entire life and I had just met him. He was a big shot Sophomore who was part of the "in" crowd. But, although I didn't know it yet, Roger had also spotted me.

Within weeks, he started meeting me between classes and walking me to my next class. He soon asked me to be his date for the Fall Festival. Of course I said "yes" even though I didn't know if my parents would allow it. When I asked Mom and Daddy, Daddy checked with a friend who knew Roger's family. Then Daddy asked my brother Charles what he knew about Roger. Charles gave his approval. So, Roger and I had our first official date in September of 1960.

Cecilia
Another Election

Dear Daddy,

Here we were again - getting ready for another presidential election. I was excited. Probably more excited than I was in the 1952 election. Our teachers at school talked about the pros and cons of each political party and of each candidate. Clearly many of them disagreed with the way you thought. I had already started to question my complete confidence in your opinions when we had the discussion about integration. Now, I questioned more as I bounced my opinions around between yours and those of my teachers.

Interest and excitement built for weeks. Everywhere, people talked about the election. At our house you talked a lot about John Fitzgerald Kennedy, the Democratic candidate. He was a young man, with a pretty wife and new ideas who was trying to become president of the United States.

According to you, he already had two strikes against him. He was a Democrat and a Catholic. You didn't think much of either one. You had hope, though, because the United States had never elected a Catholic president.

Kennedy was running against Richard Nixon, the current Vice President, a Republican. For the first time ever, presidential debates were broadcast on television. Kennedy was young and handsome. He spoke with strength and confidence. He presented himself well. Nixon, older and less polished, wasn't flattered by television. In the debate, Nixon claimed that Kennedy was too young and inexperienced to deal with serious issues of the day. Kennedy rebutted by claiming that a major issue, foreign policy, was not being handled effectively under the current Republican Administration. And so it went, back and forth. I doubt that the debates changed many minds.

Conservative protestants were frightened by Kennedy's religion. They were afraid that if Kennedy were elected, he would be too heavily influenced by the Pope and by Catholicism. Many, including you and Mom prayed for the election of Nixon. You were Southern Bapists who had strong disagreements with Catholicism. I didn't share that concern. I was attracted by the Catholic Religion when we first moved to Cecilia and made Catholic friends. "How could their religion be so bad?" I thought. It felt a little strange not to completely agree with you but I hadn't decided yet who I wanted to win this election.

On Tuesday, November 8, 1960, the election was finally held. After voting, You and Mom came home and watched election returns all day. You decided the vote was too close to call that night so you and Mom went on to bed. You would have to wait until tomorrow.

On Wednesday morning, the day after the election, I went off to school still not knowing who had won the election. Roger and I met as usual in the bleachers of Howevalley High School and waited for the first bell to call us to class.

"Who do you think will win the election?" I asked Roger.

"I hope Nixon does. Dad says that it would be bad for our country if a Catholic was elected president," Roger answered.

"That's what my Daddy says, too. But I don't understand why everyone is so against a Catholic president. I think it will be kind of exciting if Kennedy wins. He seems like he's really smart and I know all the women think he's good-looking."

Just about that time the bell rang calling us to class. I realized later that Roger hadn't told me whether he agreed with his Dad or not. I still don't know for sure. My guess is that he was rooting for Nixon just like both of our Dads.

At the end of the school day, I could hardly wait to get home. I had become excited about politics in 1952 when I first went with you to vote. At that time I was sure you knew everything. I didn't question your judgment or your choice of a president. But, I was in high school now and had listened to my teachers for weeks. I knew that many of them were rooting for Kennedy. I had been exposed to Catholics in our neighborhood and didn't believe they were bad or evil. I started to think, at times, like my teachers.

The 1960 election was the first time I can remember disagreeing with you – or at least it was the first time I'd expressed that disagreement out loud. I was becoming my own person. That election was a significant event in my growing up. I realized that I could disagree with you and Mom and still be okay.

Cecilia
What Were We Thinking?

Dear Jim,

After Roger and I had been dating for a while, he became like a part of our family. He would come to our house in Cecilia and hang out all afternoon just to get some of Mom's home cooking. He even liked the strawberry-rhubarb pie she served him once.

Roger also met and liked you and Zorada. Do you remember the time we came to Hodgenville to see you? It must have been in the summer of 1961. You took Roger for a ride on your motorcycle. Zorada and I took your car out in the country to practice driving.

Zorada had driven some around the farm where her family lived but she had never driven on public roads and had never tried to get a driver's license. I had never even sat behind the steering wheel of a car. Looking back, I wonder "What were we thinking?"

As I remember it, all we were thinking about was that we both wanted to learn to drive. So, after you and

Roger took off on the motorcycle, Zorada and I took off in the car. I can't remember the details of what the car looked liked, where it was parked, or anything else. It must have been parked facing the street, though, or we would never have been able to get it out of the driveway. You see, neither of us knew how to back up.

Zorada knew a place out in the country where there would not be much traffic and where the roads were well maintained. We decided to drive there. Everything seemed to go well. Zorada drove a while and had no problems.

But, I also wanted to drive. Soon we came to a spot where another gravel road intersected the one we were on. We had no idea what that road led to but Zorada turned right on the road. She drove a bit further and then pulled off to the side. "It's your turn, Sissy," she said. "Come around to this side." I did like she said and walked around the car, then slid in under the steering wheel. I could barely reach the gas and brake pedals with my short legs.

Thankfully the car had an automatic transmission so we didn't have to manipulate a clutch. I was only about 5'1" tall and had to sit up really straight and strain to see over the steering wheel. I waited for Zorada to get in on the passenger side then carefully put the car in drive and began slowly moving straight ahead. "This is easy," I thought. "Nothing to it." Zorada and I crept along about five miles per hour, joking and laughing.

Quickly we found out where this road led. Straight to a farmer's cattle barn. But to get to the barn, you had to open a large gate. We didn't want to go any farther. We didn't know if the farmer might come out with a gun or if an angry bull might come around the barn and charge us. So, we knew we had to back up and turn around. The road was wide enough and graveled but neither Zorada nor I knew how to reverse. "It can't be that hard," Zorada said. Trade places with me again and I will turn the car around. "You can stand back and let me know if I'm getting off the gravel. The last thing we need to do is to get hung up out here."

I turned the car off and got out. Zorada took her place in the driver's seat. She started the car and put it in reverse. I tried to direct her so that she didn't get off the gravel. But for some reason, I didn't seem to be doing a good job of directing. Zorada went forward and then backward and then forward and backward again, making no progress in getting turned around. It was starting to get dark and we didn't know what we were going to do. Remember this was way before the time of cell phones.

We couldn't call you and we weren't about to open that gate and try to find someone to help us. Both Zorada and I tried to act brave but we were both getting a little nervous. Finally you and Roger came looking for us. You got off the motorcycle and turned the car around. Zorada drove back to the house while you and Roger followed on your motorcycle.

We made it home safely and neither you nor Roger "fussed" at us. You probably did laugh a lot behind our backs. That was a fun day and maybe a little scary. Zorada and I did each finally get a driver's license. But, on that day, what in the world were we thinking?

Jeffersontown, Kentucky
2016

Dear Daddy,

Recently someone asked me to write about what a perfect day would be for me. I immediately thought, I'll write about my father. Though you have been dead for 50 years, I often sense your presence and feel as though we are having a conversation. I used to think about you in a negative sense. You had a quick and hot temper. You were never violent but would frequently yell at Mom or one of the boys – most often at Hubert. At times, as a child, I thought that we'd all be happier if you just left.

But, on my perfect day, as I wrote and conversed in my mind, I uncovered a different Dad - one who had been there all along.

I uncovered the Dad who taught me to play checkers and Rook, the Dad who brought home the big city (Louisville) newspapers and read and discussed them with me, the Dad who had a keen interest in the world around him, especially politics and sports. On my perfect day, I remembered that this Dad taught me to work and to play with enthusiasm. I remembered the sound of his voice as he "shot the moon" in Rook and laughed even when he didn't make his bid. I uncovered the Dad who spanked me only once in my entire life and the one who cried real tears as Roger and I left to go to Oklahoma to start a new life.

On my perfect day, after writing about you, I'd shut down my writing for the day. I would take a walk around the neighborhood breathing in the beauty of fall while integrating my recent thoughts with my previous ones. I'd arrive back at the house with a more complete understanding of my father and with a more positive outlook.

While James Taylor's music played in the background, I'd prepare supper for our grandsons who would soon be joining us for the evening. When the grandchildren arrived and supper was over, I'd say, "Boys, let me tell you about my dad, your great-grandfather."

Jeffersontown, Kentucky
2015

Dear Daddy,

When I was growing up, I always thought of myself as more like Mom than like you. The older I get, however, I realize I was wrong. In fact most of my adult personality and interests I can trace straight back to you and your influence.

As a child, I was frightened by your outbursts of temper that seemingly came out of nowhere. I never asked you or Mom what made you so angry. Your anger was mostly directed at Mom - never at Nora or me. As with many other puzzling subjects, I wish we all could have talked more about your anger and what caused it. I wonder even now.

One possibility is that you had taken too many nips from the bottle you always carried in the trunk of your car. Yes, I knew about it and knew that as the boys got older you sometimes let them have a nip as well. I know that you were not an alcoholic and I appreciate that you respected

Mom enough not to bring liquor into the house.

If it wasn't alcohol, what was it that brought out the anger? I try to understand but without you here to speak, I can only speculate. Did it have to do with Milton – with the way he lived his life or the way he died in the electric chair? I have newspaper clippings that describe his arrest and trial and execution. I have court transcripts that tell of the trial and of your appealing his conviction and losing. The horror of losing your first born son in this way doesn't escape me. Who would not have been angry?

I just wish, though, that you and I had talked about Milton. You could have told me about his younger life and what a cute little boy he was. You could have told me about how you dealt with all the pain of losing him.

I used to wonder why our family never had much money. I knew you worked hard to support us. A few years ago, I asked Hubert why we were so poor as we were growing up. He said it was because you spent everything you had, and everything you could borrow to pay for Milton's defense. He said you never could get out from under all that debt.

None of us children suffered from growing up in poverty. As we watched you and Mom, we learned a strong work ethic. As we worked beside you, we learned that family members help each other. And, we learned many, many skills that helped us become self sufficient and resilient.

You and Mom created a strong family. My only regret is that we didn't talk more – about events and opinions – about pain and grief.

You were so smart, one of the smartest people I've ever known, though you only had a 5th grade education. You had a quick mind that could do math almost instantly. You could look at a house and calculate very closely the amount of roofing that would be required to roof it.

You had a keen interest in many things: sports, politics, people, general news, and, you passed those interests on to me. I know that you were disappointed when I dropped out of high school but you did live to see me go back and finish only four years later. I am so glad that you were at my graduation. I hope you know that you raised a "life-long learner." I went on to earn three college degrees and became an educator, a teacher and a program manager. You would be very proud.

I inherited intelligence from you and, because of you, gained an interest in people and in the world around me.

Do you remember watching wrestling, boxing and baseball on television? You particularly liked watching "The Golden Gloves," a program that featured young boys boxing. That one little boy that you liked so much, Cassius

Clay, grew up to be Muhammad Ali, one of the world's best known boxers and an influential presence throughout most of the world.

I could never understand your fascination with wrestling nor boxing but I did learn to like baseball. During the World Series each year you'd have me watch the games while you were at work. You worked the second shift and could not be home to watch them yourself. The next day, I'd give you a report on the game. Who had pitched, who had made errors, who had lost and who had won. What a learning experience it was for me to read the newspaper and watch sports and then discuss them with you.

You also liked to play checkers and taught me to be a tough competitor. I don't believe I could ever beat you but I learned to play well enough that I could take down any other competitor.

The time I spent with you and the delight you took in my ability to learn are among my best memories of childhood. When I was a little older, about 12 as I remember, you taught me to play Rook. I learned from the best how to bid, make trumps, fake out my opponents and have fun playing. Since Rook was played as partners against partners, I would be paired up with either you, Alma, or Ernest. Most often, it was with you.

You hated to lose but never expressed anger at me if I misplayed. Instead, you'd explain what I could have done better. You taught me to count cards as they were played so I'd be aware of how many of each suit were still out. You taught me not to play a "pointer" card if my opponents were most probably holding something that would catch it. You taught me to bid and to take calculated chances.

Because you hated to lose, you'd shoot the moon (meaning you and your partner had to take every trick or lose the game) while holding a very weak hand. Many times you'd pick up just what you needed from the "kitty" (the last five cards left at the end of each deal). If you didn't get what you needed from the kitty, you'd often "hit" your partner's hand. I hated to lose as much as you so didn't like for you to shoot the moon when I was your partner. More often than not though, you'd pull us through. I soon learned to "shoot the moon" myself. It was always better to give yourself a chance to win than to play timidly and let the other team run the show. This was a valuable lesson.

In life, I have tried to live boldly and give myself a chance to win.

Cecilia
I Wish We Could Have Talked...

Dear Mom,

You were a loving and kind mother but I wish we could have talked more...

"I was afraid this would happen," you said to me after I came home from a trip to Virginia after finishing 5th grade. What did you think happened? Did you know that I had worn shorts and pedal pushers which we were never allowed to wear at home? Did you know that I had sipped part of a beer just to see how it tasted? Did you know that I had gone to a barn dance and loved every minute of it? That trip was a wonderful experience for me. I saw many new places, even Washington, D.C.. I met new people and tasted new foods.

"What do you think happened? Did I do something wrong?" I wish I had asked. "Are you talking about the times he came into my room and asked me to do things and then told me not to tell anyone?" I thought he was my friend. But, what he did when he came to my room didn't feel right. It didn't feel like something a friend would do.

Soon after the trip, I started noticing changes in my body. I know now that they were the natural changes that come in puberty. But, we hadn't talked about what happens to a girl's body as she matures. The changes frightened me.

Because we never talked about any of those things, I spent my entire 6th grade thinking I was pregnant. If I had talked to you, I would have known that I was not. I wouldn't have made up stories to tell my classmates about why I might be absent for a long time.

You were a loving mother and if you had known what I was experiencing, I know your heart would have broken. I don't know exactly why we couldn't talk. You went around a lot with tears in your eyes. Daddy would be as sweet as could be with you one day and the next day "go off" and yell at you. We never talked about that either. If we had talked openly, maybe we both would have been happier.

There seemed to be a pattern in our family not to discuss sensitive or difficult topics. Instead, each person handled difficult situations and difficult emotions alone. It was as though if we didn't talk about them, they would go away. But, they didn't go away. Not long after the Virginia experience, I became the victim of another abuser.

*****

His name was Fred Rainey. He was a doctor who lived in Elizabethtown, Kentucky. He was a former president of the Kentucky Medical Association and was well known for his civic activities. And, he pled guilty in 1990 to 50 counts of rape, sodomy and sexual abuse committed over a period of 31 years and involving seven juveniles – five of them his patients.

I was one of his victims. My abuse started in 1958 when I was a naïve 13 years old. Mom took me to Rainey for strep throat. During the exam, with no one else in the room, he touched me inappropriately. When the exam was over, he asked if I'd like to work for him, babysitting or answering phones. Then he asked Mom and she gave her permission. Rainey said that when he needed me, he would call first and then pick me up to go to his house or office.

The first time he picked me up, I was nervous and excited. I thought I could talk to him about the changes I'd been worried about. I couldn't talk to anyone else about them. I worried that they might mean that I was going to have a baby. I would have a chance to talk to a doctor now and he would take care of me.

That first time, he drove to his office where he let me in and showed me the phone. "Just take a message if anyone calls. Tell them I'll return their call later," he said. Then he left me alone in the office for about 2 hours and the phone never rang. When he came back, he asked if there had been any calls and then took out his wallet and gave me some bills. We went out to his car to go home.

Instead of taking me straight home, he drove to the driveway of an abandoned house and parked. Then, he raped me. After he finished, he cleaned me and said, "Don't say anything to your mother about this." I couldn't talk to my mother about it and I'm sure Rainey knew it. He knew how to pick his victims.

For the next two years, I continued to "work" for him. In between calls, I told myself not to go again. I prayed for strength to say, "No." I felt that what was happening was wrong but I couldn't talk to anyone about it. I had no way of understanding. Then he would call again and I'd go.

Looking at me, everyone saw the same child I'd always been, maturing and becoming a teenager. I pasted on a smile and did the things I'd always done – attended church activities, made good grades at school, obeyed my parents…But what everyone saw was the pretend me.

I crawled into myself and spent more and more time alone in my room with books. My real self curled up like a roly-poly for protection. Often, I sat at the kitchen table crying for no apparent reason. When anyone asked what was wrong, I couldn't say. I only knew that I was overcome by sadness that I didn't understand and couldn't explain.

I wish we could have talked.

Tasting the Truth

One of my favorite quotes by William Butler Yeats, the English poet says, "We taste and feel and see the truth. We do not reason ourselves into it."

Abuse changed me. For years, I tried to reason it away. I learned early on to keeps secrets. I spent years having difficulty relating honestly to people and forming true friendships. I retreated into books and intellect. I put on a mask and faced the world with a smile.

It took many years before I awoke one morning and said, "That SOB raped me." I finally felt, and saw, and tasted the truth. I finally accepted my life as it was – abuse and all – and it was a pretty good life.

Now, I celebrate survival. I celebrate success in accomplishing educational and professional goals. I celebrate friends and the ability to be open and honest knowing that they love me as I am. Most of all, I celebrate family: a husband who supports me, two amazing sons who have families of their own, all of my nieces, nephews, cousins, and other extended family.

The fabric of our family is multihued and strong – much like the patchwork quilt covering my bed.

About the Author

Jean was born in Cub Run, Kentucky. She attended school at several schools in rural Kentucky before graduating from West Hardin High School in 1966.

She attended Eastern Kentucky University, Jefferson County Community College and the University of Louisville where she obtained a BA in English, a Master's in Secondary Education and a Rank 1 in Educational Administration. She is a retired teacher and program manager currently living in Louisville, Kentucky.

Jean is a lifelong learner with a love of reading and writing. She began writing poetry and short essays at a young age. She has published poetry in small literary magazines; public relations materials in *Central Communique*, a newspaper for teachers; opinion articles and short essays in the Louisville *Courier Journal*; and, personality profiles in *Picture This!*, a fine art auction catalog.

In this, Jean's first book, she tells stories about growing up during the 1940's & 1950's in various places in rural Kentucky.

www.ingramcontent.com/pod-product-compliance
Lightning Source LLC
Chambersburg PA
CBHW032031290426
44110CB00012B/763